What people are saying about *Letters Home*:

Nothing gives a more realistic and insightful picture into history than personal letters written home to family. In sharing the letters by his uncle when serving as a US Navy chief mechanic, Eric Ehrke offers us extraordinary insight into the historically significant years of 1918–1919—a rare first-person account of the US Navy's seaplane infancy during WWI and the Spanish Influenza pandemic.

Letters Home is deeply personal and intimate, but readers will relate to and be inspired by Arthur Ehrke's dreams and longings, his passion for duty, his love of home. We must thank the woman who saved his letters in a shoebox under the bed and Eric Ehrke for completing the account begun by his mother. The letters, photos, and personal observations provide a snapshot into a great American story and make for a compelling read.

—Jennifer Read Hawthorne, co-author, #1 New York Times bestseller
Chicken Soup for the Woman's Soul and author, *Life as a Prayer: Poems*

Through his uncle's letters home, Eric Ehrke has brought to life Arthur Ehrke's experiences as a chief seaplane mechanic in the US Navy during World War I. The writing is heart-warming and sincere, and the historical photos provide a picture into life during the worldwide Spanish Influenza pandemic.

—Terri Arthur, RN, award-winning author of
Fatal Decision: Edith Cavell, World War I Nurse

Eric Ehrke has put together a fascinating first-hand account of our country's WWI war efforts by sharing personal letters and documents from his uncle, Arthur Ehrke, who was a sea-plane test engineer during the war. Additionally, Eric displayed numerous personal and archived pictures related to the stories told in the letters producing a visual context to what was happening. The combination of letters and pictures gives the reader deeper and very intimate insight into the real-life human side of this important American historical event.

—Richard Grothaus, PhD

Eric Ehrke has crafted a gripping retrospect of the short but productive life of his uncle, Arthur Ehrke. Arthur was one of the many unsung heroes during the infancy of naval aviation. The book describes the challenges and sacrifices they all faced. The book also presents a time capsule of an era (1917-1919) including the end of a World War and the start of a pandemic known as the Spanish Flu.

—Lauren Lauritch, Educator 40 plus years

LETTERS HOME FROM A WWI SEAPLANE TEST MECHANIC

How Arthur Ehrke Lived and Died on the Wings of Aeroplanes

Arthur Ehrke (1899–1919).

Also by Eric Ehrke:

The Promise of Wholeness: Cultivating Inner Peace, Mindfulness, and Love in a Divided World
Published by Rowman & Littlefield Publishers
(February 8, 2019)
www.Rowman.com

LETTERS HOME FROM A WWI SEAPLANE TEST MECHANIC:

How Arthur Ehrke Lived and Died on the Wings of Aeroplanes

ERIC EHRKE

Milwaukee, Wisconsin

Copyright © 2023 by Eric Ehrke
All rights reserved

Photo credits are provided with individual images.

Published by
HenschelHAUS Publishing, Inc.
www.henschelHAUSbooks.com
Milwaukee, Wisconsin

ISBN (PB): 978159598-966-6
ISBN (HC): 978159598-967-3
LCCN: 2023941831

Cover photo of seaplane: This file is a work of a sailor or employee of the U.S. Navy, taken or made as part of that person's official duties. As a work of the U.S. federal government, it is in the public domain in the United States.

In 1921, the Aviation Rigger rating was established, and in 1926 the rating was officially changed to Aviation Machinist's Mate Rating. The WWI Machinist's Mate Insignia looked similar to the design above in Art's photos, so the propeller/wing design is included in the book.

Printed in the United States of America

DEDICATION

This book is dedicated to my uncle, Arthur Ehrke, whose letters home provide a wonderful window into a gentler time, when the written word was the only way to reveal one's heartfelt love and passion from a distance.

Courtesy of the Naval History and Heritage Command

TABLE OF CONTENTS

Foreword i

Prologue 1

Introduction 5

Chapter 1: I was Only a Volunteer 7

Chapter 2: The Great Lakes Training Station in 1918 19

Chapter 3: The Spanish Influenza and
          Philadelphia's Naval Aircraft Factory 39

Chapter 4: The Spanish Influenza Wanes and a US Seaplane
          First to Cross the Atlantic 87

Chapter 5: Arthur Ehrke's Untimely Death 153

Chapter 6: Perspectives and Observations 185

Epilogue 195

Appendix 1: Chronology of Art's Letters 199

Appendix 2: Dr. Cauffman's Secret Advice 203

Appendix 3: Additional Family Documents 213

Acknowledgments 227

About the Author 229

Foreword

Robert M. Lawn, Captain, USN (Retired)
Senior Fellow, National Defense University (Retired)
Colonel – Pilot, Commemorative Air Force
Licensed Private Pilot

Are you ready for an adventure? *Letters Home* takes you on a rapid descent 100 years ago into aviation's history as the United States entered World War I. A true story, it is superbly presented by Eric Ehrke about the short life and path of a young man, his uncle, Arthur Ehrke, and the world of global upheavals in which he lived. Arthur's story is woven as layers of insights so that the reader can relate to the maturing growth of a young man during troubling times.

This record of life and Navy career is the result of the continual exchange of written letters and historical records preserved by his family. It begins with a young man's search through personal life choices in West Allis, Wisconsin. This city is important for it was the center of the expanding metal-machining industry of the young United States. And within this geographical area was a stable, hard-working social structure, a skilled labor market, a solid community and national ethic, and an expanding industrial/economic class. It was within this environment that Arthur's life was molded, coupled by a strong family nucleus.

Global affairs and issues of state always play as significant influencers to personal choices and career paths. These two influencers were huge: the global impact of the Spanish Influenza and the initiation of World War I. The path that Arthur followed was of national service, which led to his career choice to pursue his machinist skill in the US Navy and seaplane aviation. Arthur's letters start at the Great Lakes Naval Training Station in 1918 just as the Spanish Influenza was about to hit the base. And his passion to excel led to his talent as a skilled

Letters Home from a WWI Seaplane Test Mechanic

Chief Mechanic at America's first Naval Aircraft Factory in Philadelphia. The selection to the rate of Chief Petty Officer in the US Navy is a significant and major personal accomplishment, demonstrating the depth of his professional character, knowledge and skill.

You are invited to consider the world in which Arthur lived and breathed. Arthur's letters and correspondence provided his attitudes to life and the norms tied to the social structure of his time. There are evidences of his focus and values molded by world affairs represented by the language use within his correspondence. You can feel his views on meaningful relationships when discussing the subject of trust. You can feel the responses when coping with the subject of death. One letter references the words "it must have been his time" when discussing the passing of a close friend. All this was transpiring during a pandemic bluntly visible to him where many friends, acquaintances, and colleagues/shipmates perished. This gives *Letters Home* a deep window through which to view the social norms and values of Arthur's generation. It demonstrates a lot of humanity's best qualities.

I have known Eric Ehrke for over 30 years as a personal integral friend and astute colleague. We initially crossed paths while attending lectures and educational sessions designed to investigate critical thinking and strategic thought practices. My career of 30-plus years in Naval Aviation, both flying and in senior command positions, offers insights into the infancy of the naval aviation community.

The early Navy seaplanes were the initial mission aircraft that eventually evolved into the P-3 Orion, in which I accumulated over 2,800 flight hours. The P-3 Orion has now been superseded by the Navy's P-8 Poseidon. Technology has exponentially advanced from visual surveillance seaplanes to multi-role flying cocoons of microelectronic hardware that can stay airborne with midair refueling. Consider the advancement of operational manuals for each aircraft component, safely equipment and safety procedures, flight and aircrew checklist, and maintenance and overhaul procedures. None of these described existed to the norm or standards acceptable to our present generation. Grabbing a plane and flying by the seat of one's pants is not an option today. But operational hazards continue to exist even today and are experienced by many pilots.

I'm no exception, having experienced an aircraft midair crash in a night-time landing pattern from an unauthorized intruding aircraft. All survived the incident and walked away, due primarily to the safety procedures, equipment, and repetitive training created by those who came before us; but the aircraft did not.

The risks within the fledgling naval aviation and Arthur's community were enormous. Only a decade stands between the Wright brothers' first flight and the first World War. Technology and practical knowledge were pushed to the limits of its time. Air crews flew without parachutes or life-support equipment, which is why so many aviators were killed during crashes. Pilots had no cockpit instrumentation, as seem in supporting photo documentation within this book. Weather forecasts for mission flying were visual guesses. And the planes were constructed of wood and glued, fabric-coated wings. Regarding the technology of the era, no two seaplanes were identical. Thus, the slang used by aviators, such as flying *on a wing and a prayer* or *it was all stick and rudder* have literally true meaning. And for Arthur, each aircraft that was built at the Naval Airplane Factory was a unique mechanical system that he had to fine-tune individually as the Chief Mechanic.

Eric's presentation is a superb demonstration of skill and love. *Letter's Home* provides a window, through their written words, how families endured during hard economic times, a global pandemic, and a national emergency. It also shows us the value of strong families, kindness within daily activity, and the lasting relationships of our human experience. I am honored to recommend unequivocally this simple yet veryheart felt expression of family and core values, all which are encompassed within the factual life of Arthur Ehrke.

Lillian and Walter Ehrke (1915).

Helen Ehrke (1978).

Walter Ehrke in uniform (1945).

PROLOGUE

My father, Walter Ehrke, was a harbor pilot of a patrol torpedo (PT) boat for the US Coast Guard during World War II. After Pearl Harbor, he volunteered to serve his country, just as his brother Arthur had during World War I, and was stationed in Milwaukee, Wisconsin.

Arthur and my father moved up the ranks into leadership roles quickly. The Navy and the love of water run deep in my family. During my childhood, every member of my father's family had a cottage on Green Lake. Glacially formed, 27 miles around and 235 feet deep, Green Lake is one of Wisconsin's most beautiful lakes.

An American patriot, my father always thought of himself as a US citizen and never mentioned his or my mother's German heritage. Loyalty was very important to my father, which is why my oldest brother, Lance A. Ehrke's, middle name is Arthur.

When I was in sixth grade, without any family prompting, Arthur was the only confirmation name I considered. My uncle Art died when my father was seven years old, four years after the picture opposite was taken. He had some big shoes to fill.

This book would not exist without the inspiration from my mother, Helen Ehrke. A master's degreed librarian and skilled genealogist, she traced both sides our family to the early 1700s. Dedicated to our family heritage, she exhausted our country's resources first then traveled to Germany to finish her work. When she heard that Aunt Dell had saved all of Arthur's letters in a shoebox under her bed for sixty years, she asked Dell if she could see them. This occurred around 1978.

A skilled typist, she read each delicate hand-written letter and faithfully typed up its contents. She surprised the family that Christmas with a complete booklet of Art's letters typed up in sequence. She featured many family pictures, most of which are included in this book. It became a smash hit not only to family members, but also to the casual

Mathilda, Della, Lillian, Arthur, and Gustav Ehrke circa 1909.
Born in 1911, my father Walter is not pictured.

reader. Since his letters provided a rare first-person account of the US Navy's seaplane infancy during WWI and the Spanish Influenza pandemic, I took my mother's book to HenschelHAUS Publishing in 2007. Kira Henschel, the owner, came to my mother's house and offered to co-publish the book, if we wrote an introductory and concluding chapter. Unfortunately, macular degeneration had taken most of my mother's eyesight by that time and she passed away in 2014. Prior to her death, my mother told me the family stories and I promised to finish the book. I inherited all of Arthur's letters and possessions since my father Walter, Aunt Dell, and Aunt Lillian had passed years prior. This book completes my mother's inspiration.

My mother always spoke about how hard Mathilda took Arthur's death in 1919. The numbers of letter's Mathilda wrote to anyone who knew her son speaks to her grief. My father, Walter Ehrke, never spoke about what it was like to lose his brother or the pressure he endured when he became the only surviving son at the tender age of seven. He did speak about how tenderly Gustav Ehrke, my grandfather, would hold me in his arms for hours while he overlooked Green Lake and I slept as a baby.

Grandpa Ehrke took a particular liking to my older brother Lance and frequently invited him to his cottage on Green Lake for weekend sleep-overs during his retirement years. Gustav Ehrke, Aunt Dell, Aunt Lill, and our family all had cottages on Green Lake in central Wisconsin. We always remained close-knit family. My aunts and uncles argued politics with great fervor during the holidays and of course, no one ever changed anyone else's mind. My mother would tease my father by saying her vote would cancel out his every election.

Gustav Ehrke died when I was only five and my grandmother passed away shortly after I was born, so most of what I learned about my grandparents and Uncle Arthur came from my mother's genealogy and the following letters.

Paranormal sensitivity may run in my family. In 1919, Arthur had a premonition the day before he died that he wouldn't see his landlord again. He felt the two pilots flying with him the next morning would never land the seaplane safely. It turns out he was right, as Art, one of pilots, and another crew member died during their crash landing.

Interestingly enough, my father had his own paranormal experience after his car crashed into an oak tree at 70 miles per hour in 1966. As the emergency workers approached the wreckage, my father had an out-of-body experience. While his body was trapped unconscious inside the car, he described how he began to float above the car and saw his crushed body wrapped around the steering wheel. Simultaneously, he heard the EMTs say to one another he was probably dead as they approached. He screamed in their ears and told them he was alive with no effect.

When the "Jaws of Life" pried open the driver's door and one of the men touched him, my father immediately flew back into his body and later woke up in the hospital. He never repeated the story in public again, but as a result, I spent many years of my life exploring paranormal phenomena. Unfortunately, most of us don't trust the information or believe it could happen.

This book of family letters is a 1918-1919 time capsule that will transport the reader to a young country during a gentler time in the later stages of World War I. Prohibition and a worldwide pandemic called the Spanish Influenza was about to affect every citizen in United States. These letters let you walk in the shoes of Arthur Ehrke, who was born over a century ago.

Letters Home from a WWI Seaplane Test Mechanic

Sit back, look at the Naval History and Heritage Command photos and imagine what it must have been like to fly the first seaplanes ever constructed during aviation's infancy. Walk on the wings of a bi-winged seaplane with built-in footpaths so a mechanic could repair an in-flight engine. Crash landings were common and test mechanics and pilots often enough ended up in the drink.

Enjoy the following letters and historical information. You will soon realize why Arthur wrote, "If you ever find me dead..." instructions on the first page of his personal notebook, which never left his possession.

INTRODUCTION

In May 1918, at the age of eighteen, Arthur Ehrke enlisted in the Navy with his best friend, Fred Eisemann. Like so many men of their time, they were afraid World War I would end before they "could see something of it." Having already apprenticed as a mechanic at Kempsmith Manufacturing before his enlistment, Arthur applied himself and became an Aircraft Machinist First Class at the Navy's Great Lakes Training Station in September 1918.

Arthur Ehrke arrived in Philadelphia right before the City of Brotherly Love was about to become the epicenter of the Spanish Influenza in United States. He decided he wasn't going to get sick and six months after arriving at our country's first naval aircraft factory, Arthur became Chief Mechanic with twenty-five seamen under him. As Chief Mechanic, the Navy sent him to the 1919 New York Liberty Loan

Postcard of the Great Lakes Training Station (1918).

Parade to promote the war effort as the US Navy prepared to make the first trans-Atlantic flight from New York's Rockaway Naval Air Station two months later.

This is a story about strong family ties and a young US Navy seaplane mechanic's letters home during aviation's infancy. How they lived and loved during the war and the worst pandemic the world had ever seen since the Black Plague is a riveting story. This is a book of pictures and letters from a gentler time where the written word was the only way to reveal one's heart and soul from a distance.

As the Chief Mechanic at Philadelphia's Naval Aircraft Factory, Arthur crash-landed many times, lost the tip of his finger, and walked on the wings of the first seaplanes the United States ever built. His death while testing a seaplane barely a year after he entered the Great Lakes Training Station devasted everyone who knew him. Fortunately, you can meet him through his own written word. His letters home from a century ago reveal the principles and values that remain timeless. I invite you to meet my uncle, my grandparents, and the people who loved them now.

Only A Volunteer

Nobody gave me a banquet,
Nobody said a kind word:
The puff of the engine, the grind of the wheels,
Made the only good-bye that I heard.
I was off to the training camp hustled.
To be trained for a dreary half year,
And then in the shuffle forgotten—
I was only a volunteer.

Why didn't I wait to be drafted,
And be led to the train by a band?
Why didn't I ask for exemption,
Oh, why did I hold my hand?
Why didn't I wait for the banquet?
Why didn't I wait to be cheered?
For the drafted man got the glory and pie,
While I merely volunteered.

Believed to have been written by Frishe, printed in
1917-1918 Logbook of the Naval Aircraft Association.

CHAPTER ONE
I WAS ONLY A VOLUNTEER

"Wars, plagues, names upon tombs tell us only what happened. But history lies in the cracks in between. In the inexplicable, invisible turns and decisions. A person saying no instead of yes. ...It is not that they had lived...but how."
—Sarah Blake, *The Guest Book*

This story starts in the nineteenth century, when a young mechanic born in 1899, test-flew the first US Navy seaplanes during the Great War as a deadly pandemic ravaged the world. Historians say duty, honor, and country are the primary reasons men and women serve their country and have done so throughout history.

From front to back: Lillian Ehrke, Adelia Ehrke, unknown friend, Arthur Ehrke, and Fred Eisemann. Fred lived across the street and enlisted in the Navy with Arthur.

This book of letters documents a year of Arthur E. Ehrke's (1899–1919) attempt to accomplish all three as a Chief Mechanic in the Naval Aircraft Factory at the Philadelphia Naval Yards during WWI. Maintaining his machines and boats, as he called them, he walked on the wings of first seaplanes ever built by the US Navy as a test flight mechanic. Like so many men of his day who came from loving families and supportive communities, the written word was the fabric that linked hearts and souls together. Thankfully, Art's older sister, Adelia, kept his letters so my uncle and family's story of how they lived and loved each other during a gentler time was preserved before his untimely death.

Arthur's letters begin on YMCA stationary near the Great Lakes Naval Training Station, but his parents, Mathilda and Gustav Ehrke, first need an introduction.

A shoe-cutter, Gustav Ehrke (1876–1956) was born in Germany, immigrated to the United States in 1886, and naturalized in 1906. In 1897, he married Mathilda Pawelke (1872–1952) and Adelia was born a year later in Milwaukee, Wisconsin. At that time, Milwaukee had a large German population, made up of those who fled their country due to social, political, and cultural upheavals in Europe. Over five million Germans immigrated to the "German Triangle," which included Cincinnati, Milwaukee, and St. Louis in the 1800s.[1] Most were farmers, artisans and laborers. When the Socialist Democratic Party was established in Milwaukee in 1897, Gustav became active in local politics. He eventually was elected to the Police and Fire Commission Board for two four-year terms. Since socialism is such a loaded word these days, the Socialist Democratic Party's 1912 Milwaukee Municipal Campaign Book's mission statement follows:

> *What is a Socialist? It is a man*
> *Who strives to formulate or aid a plan*
> *To better earth's conditions. It is he*
> *Who, having ears to hear and eyes to see,*
> *Is neither deaf nor blind when might, rough-shod,*

---

[1] Library of Congress. *The Germans in America.*
https://www.loc.gov/rr/european/imde/germchr.html

Treads down the privileges and rights which God
Means for all men; the right to toil,
To breathe pure air, to till the fertile soil-
To live, to love, to woo, to wed,
And earn for hungry mouths their meed of bread.
The Socialist is he who claims no more
Than his own share from generous Nature's store;
But he asks, and asks, too, that no other
Shall claim the share of any weaker brother,
And brand him beggar in his own domain,
To glut a mad, inordinate lust for gain.
The Socialist is one who holds the best
Of all God's gifts is toil, the second, rest.
He asks that all men learn the sweets of labor,
And no idler fatten off his neighbor;
That all men be allowed their share of leisure,
Nor thousands slave that one may seek his pleasure.
Who on the Golden Rule shall dare insist-
Behold him, the modern Socialist.
—Ella Wheeler Wilcox

An activist herself, Mathilda Ehrke was a founding member of NAIN Ladies Aid in 1914, a Lutheran organization with a unique name. In the bible, Nain was the village in Galilee where Jesus comforted a grieving widow by raising her son from the dead. According to the canonical gospels, Jesus raised three people from the dead during his lifetime. Lazarus is a well-known story but the resurrection of the son from Nain focuses on how much this helped the grieving mother, who also was a widow. Upon witnessing this miracle, the amazed crowd concluded, "God has come to help his people." A lifelong Ladies Aid volunteer and nurturing mother, upon her passing a memorial was sent to the NIAN Reconstructed Church. After Arthur died when his seaplane crashed into the Delaware River, she struggled mightily.

Arthur's three siblings were Adelia (1898–1994), Lillian (1904–1998), and Walter (1911–1989). As a psychotherapist, I've noticed how often throughout my career that children become mirror images of who their parents were and what they *did*—not what they *said* or hoped to accomplish. Everyone one of Gustav and Mathilda's children made the world a better place during their lives, no doubt due their modeling.

Arthur's story starts when he enlisted in Navy in May of 1918 and was stationed at the Great Lakes Naval Training Station.

A Brief History of Great Lakes Naval Training Station

The first US Naval Training Station was built at Newport, Rhode Island, in 1881 and was a novel concept at the time. Previously, every enlisted sailor would report directly to his ship. However, after the Spanish-American War, President Teddy Roosevelt and the Navy decided in 1902 a second training facility was needed. After carefully examining where the best sailors came from within the country, the seasoned experts made a surprising discovery. The Navy brass concluded that the best sailors came from the Midwest. After the political

The busy train depot at the Great Lakes Naval Station in Waukegan, IL during WWI.
(Courtesy of the National Archives College Park, Maryland)

wrangling eventually settled, a 172-acre wilderness site forty miles north of Chicago was chosen.

The Great Lakes Naval Station is located on Lake Michigan and its original thirty-nine buildings with a capacity to house 1,500 men was completed in 1911. Wildly popular and completely supported by the residents of Waukegan and Chicago, things started slowly at first. Even though World War I began in 1914, barely 2,000 recruits were trained annually at Great Lakes before United States entered the war in 1917. Like a mighty locomotive, Great Lakes took time to get a head of steam but wartime urgency changed everything.

By April 1917, the first 9,000 recruits were divided into "regimentes" of 1,726 sailors and housed in tent cities and local facilities until more buildings could be built. Called "The Fighting Tradesmen," a crew of 1,200 men routinely used 1,000 pounds of nails a day to build more barracks. By the war's end, 125,000 sailors trained at Great Lakes and the Naval Station grew to 776 buildings. Dignitaries, sightseers, and families of the recruits routinely visited to listen to the Great Lakes Naval Revue, which included comedian Benjamin Kubelsy (later known as Jack Benny). John Philip Sousa and his Great Lakes Band Battalion played there and toured the country to sell war bonds and support war charities. The Great Lakes football team, whose lineup included George Halas, a future Chicago Bears player/coach icon, won the 1919 Rose Bowl.

A darling project of the press and local residents, hundreds of unpaid volunteers worked at Great Lakes to support the war effort. After viewing an air show and a precision drilling demonstration, a reporter from the *St. Louis Post-Dispatch* gushed, "It is not only that faces, throats, and arms are tanned to the gleam of precious metal, and that the treasure of youth, divine youth at the zenith of its physical perfection, glistens through close-fitting summer uniforms, from lithe sinew and resilient muscle, like incandescent wire through its globe of glass." Be still my heart. This quote may say more about the reporter than the lithe lads at Great Lakes, however.

The Great Lakes Naval Station was within walking distance of Waukegan, which was its strength, but unfortunately also became its weakness when the Spanish Influenza arrived in 1918. A brief history of what Art described in his letters as the *Spanish grippe* follows.

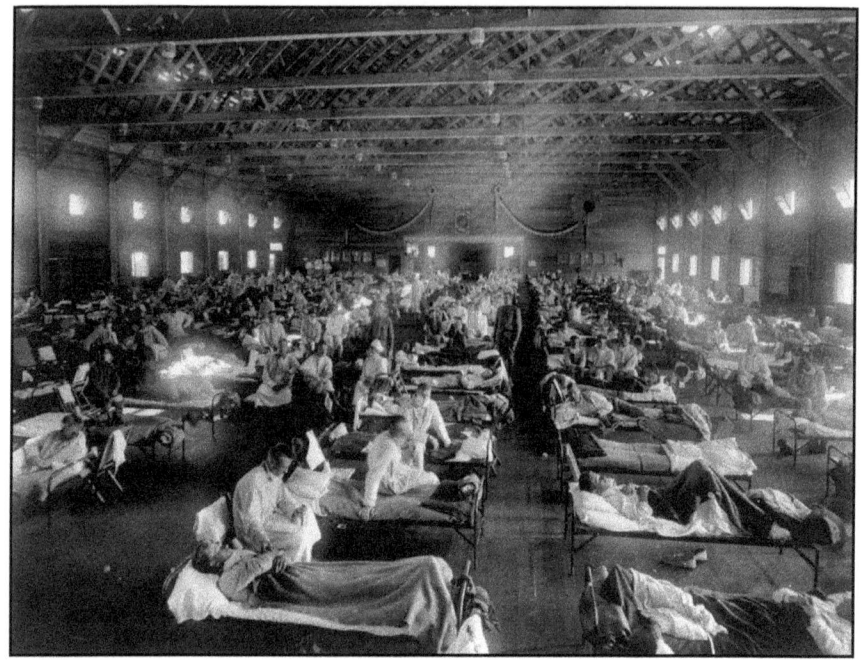

A temporary hospital in Camp Funston, Kansas, during the 1918-19 influenza epidemic. (Courtesy of the Otis Historical Archives, National Museum of Health and Medicine)

CENSORSHIP AND THE SPANISH INFLUENZA

Historians say the first documented case of the Spanish Influenza occurred in January 1918 in Haskell County, Kansas. It spread to the local army base in early March and within days, 522 men at Camp Funston reported sick. Since Funston was a major training ground for the American Expeditionary Forces, it quickly spread from Kansas due to troop deployments to our eastern military camps. Our soldiers eventually infected our allies and enemies in Europe, although some historians suggest it originated in China and spread to England and France.

More importantly, the epidemic had three distinct waves in the Midwest and along the East Coast. The fourth wave affected the rest of the world more than United States. The first wave, which occurred during the first half of 1918, resulted in no quarantines and was not as devastating in America as it was in Europe. Due to the squalid and cramped conditions of trench warfare, the pandemic greatly added to everyone's misery. Eventually, three-quarters of the French troops, half of the British troops, and 900,000 German soldiers contracted the disease.

Censors minimized and sometimes lied about the health crisis within each warring nation due to the war. However, Spain was a neutral country without censorship. Since roughly 80 percent of its population contracted the disease, every news agency around the world reported its devastating effects within Spain. Even though the influenza epidemic started in the United States, this is the reason we refer to the WWI pandemic as the Spanish Influenza today.

Estimates state that about one third of the world's population became infected and 50 million people died during the pandemic. Six hundred and seventy-five thousand Americans died from the Spanish Influenza, most between the ages 19 and 42 years old. Every doctor and scientist throughout the world mistakenly thought all flus were caused by bacteria. This influenza was a virus, which was something totally new to modern medicine at the time. The scientific community never really developed an effective vaccine or treatment to treat the disease.

The second wave of the pandemic occurred during the last half of 1918. It was the deadliest wave and military bases were hotbeds. The common flu was a known malady at that time. It lasted for a few days and occasionally was lethal to the old and infirmed. The Spanish Influenza, in its lethal form, turned victims bluish-black due to oxygen deprivation, fevers of 104 to 106 F° ensued, and eventually people drowned in their own body fluids. Additionally, the virus triggered secondary health issues, often pneumonia. What made matters worse, healthy people between 15 and 40 years old were hit the hardest, besides those with immune issues 65 and older.

A children's jump rope rhyme heard nationwide during the height of the pandemic was:

> *I had a little bird, and its name was Enza*
> *Opened the window and In-flu-enza.*

Hard-hit communities passed mask and quarantine orders. Due to the war effort and patriotism, most people wore masks and followed health orders. Unfortunately, the gauze masks never really helped much since the virus easily passed through the loose fabric. Civilians who resisted wearing masked were called "slackers." Violators of local mask ordinances usually paid a fine of $5 or had their names published in the local paper on the slacker list. In one of his letters, Art describes being given a shot of brown stuff in his nose before leaving on liberty. Military bases at that time thought an iodine nose spray would offer protection. It did not work, like everything else the medical community tried.

Dubbed "the unwelcome visitor" by the camp newspaper, the Spanish Influenza hit the Great Lakes Naval Station in September 1918. Eventually, seven nurses, who followed medical guidelines, succumbed to the disease at Great Lakes by the end of the year. Martin Birkham, a YMCA volunteer where Art rented a room just a few weeks earlier said it swept in "like the Black Plague."

During September until December, Wisconsin had 103,000 people come down with the disease. The Great Lakes commander minimized the epidemic to the local press, as was the custom of every warring nation during WWI. Regrettably, from September 12th to October 11th, 1918, the Great Lakes Training Station suffered through 9,623 influenza cases and 924 deaths. Leo Bouton, who had recovered from the influenza, sent a letter with the following sentence tucked inside that somehow got by the censors:

> *"The people on the outside don't get the news and happenings as they really are, they don't publish them as they figure it discourages and makes relatives of the enlisted men here feel uneasy, as no doubt it does."*[2]

Liberty ended for enlisted men at Great Lakes on September 19th, 1918. But the commander continued the practice of authorizing leaves for convalescent cases, who were "depressed to the point of loss of interest in all things." While the men were quarantined, the Great Lake morgues were stacked to the ceiling and trucks took away the dead

---

[2] Jeff Nichols, "The Ghosts of Great Lakes," *City Life/Chicago Reader*, 4-6-20

Best friends, Fred Eisemann and Arthur Ehrke enlisted in the Navy together in 1918. (Ehrke family photo)

every evening. This epidemic devastated Great Lakes during my Uncle Art's basic training, but he was young and full of life. He never got the Spanish Influenza, even though he arrived in Philadelphia in October 1918, where the influenza was even more lethal.

Art's take on the war and the influenza truly reflected his attitude on life. He was on a mission to be the best aviation mechanic he could be and assured his mother that he wasn't going to get sick. When you read the following letters, I invite you to assess the sense of community and commitment to the greater good that they embody. I hope that some of their love and light provide a warm reflection for the reader to enjoy. Sit down and take your time to read these letters just as they did to write them a century ago. Let your heart and soul be filled by their humanity and family values as they loved and lost.

Good deeds live on in the hearts and minds of those who remember. In May 1918, Art enlisted in the Navy with his best friend Fred Eisemann, who is referenced frequently throughout the year. Like so many men of that time, they were afraid the war would end before they "could see something of it." Art's letters begin in July when he lived at a YMCA near the Great Lakes Training Station during his basic training to become a naval aviation mechanic.

Before he enlisted in the Navy, Arthur worked as a machinist at the Kempsmith Manufacturing Company. Art obviously caught the attention of the president of the company because a few days after he enlisted the president of the company wrote him with prophetic advice.

JOHN GOETZ, Vice Prest.
E. E. LEASON, Asst. Treasurer
PAUL E. THOMAS, President and Treasurer
F. WOLLAEGER JR Secretary
PETER LOWE, Asst Secretary

THE KEMPSMITH MANUFACTURING CO.

MANUFACTURERS OF

KEMPSMITH

MILLING MACHINES

Cable Address: KEMPSMITH MILWAUKEE
Codes
A.B.C. 5TH ED. and LIEBERS
WESTERN UNION UNIVERSAL ED.
WESTERN UNION 5 LETTER ED.

QUOTATIONS SUBJECT TO CHANGE WITHOUT NOTICE.
ADDRESS ALL CORRESPONDENCE TO THE COMPANY

MILWAUKEE, U.S.A.

May 24th, 1918.

Dear Mr. Ehrke.

If you have not already applied for insurance under the Government's plan for men in the Army and Navy, I want to urge you to apply at once. You can afford to take a policy for the maximum amount, $10,000. With the Government itself bearing the whole cost of the war, this is the most advantageous insurance that was ever offered.

The benefits are of the most real sort. If you die while in the service, this insurance will bring payments your beneficiary receives from the Government to the amount corresponding with American standards of living. If you are disabled, you will receive payments according to the same standards. When your service has ended, you will be able to continue the insurance with the government even though you would not be insured by a company.

In every event this insurance represents an opportunity that no man of responsibility or any business sense can afford to miss. The opportunity is lost unless application is made before April 12th, 1918 or 120 days after a man enters the service, if this period carries the time beyond April 12th.

The advantages make the Government's insurance equally indispensable for married and unmarried men. An unmarried man is just as likely as a married man to become disabled and is just as certain to want insurance after the war is over.

Please let me know whether or not you have applied for insurance, and for how much.

As you will know, the beneficiaries for the Government's insurance are limited by law. Consequently, in writing to you I have no interest in your insurance. But I have every interest in your welfare, and on that account I am asking you, as earnestly as I know how, to act at once, if you have not already applied for insurance.

Very truly yours,

THE KEMPSMITH MFG. CO.
President.

The previous letter from the president of the manufacturing company where Arthur worked when he enlisted provides a glimpse of a thoughtful leader during gentler times. Art bought the insurance but lied about his age, which caused a significant problem for his parents after his death, when they had to prove they were his beneficiaries.

The United States of America

TREASURY DEPARTMENT
BUREAU OF WAR RISK INSURANCE
WASHINGTON, D. C.

CERTIFICATE No. 2947298

Date insurance effective May 27 1918

This Certifies That Arthur Ernest Ehrke

has applied for insurance in the amount of $ 10,000 , payable in case of death or total permanent disability in monthly installments of $ 57.50

Subject to the payment of the premiums required, this insurance is granted under the authority of an Act amending "An Act entitled 'An Act to authorize the establishment of a Bureau of War Risk Insurance in the Treasury Department,' approved September 2, 1914, and for other purposes," approved October 6, 1917, and subject in all respects to the provisions of such Act, of any amendments thereto, and of all regulations thereunder, now in force or hereafter adopted, all of which, together with the application for this insurance, and the terms and conditions published under authority of the Act, shall constitute the contract.

McAdoo
Secretary of the Treasury.

William C. DeLanoy
Director of the Bureau of War Risk Insurance.

Countersigned at Washington, D. C., _____
Registrar.

FORM 711

Great Lakes Naval Training Station Parade Grounds circa 1918.
(NH S-361—Courtesy of the Naval History and Heritage Command)

Trainee's Quarters at the Great Lakes Training Station, 1917.
(S-147-B.02—Courtesy of the Naval History and Heritage Command)

Aerial view of the Great Lakes Training Station.
(NH S-361 A.01—Courtesy of the Naval History and Heritage Command)

Chapter Two
The Great Lakes Training Station in 1918

Like so many men who serve their country during war, Art wanted to see action. With a single-minded purpose, he focused on becoming the best aviation mechanic possible. Since he worked at Kempsmith Manufacturing at age seventeen, Art already knew a lot about lathes and industrial machinery. Eighteen years old at the time he enlisted, Arthur inflated his age by three years to gain credibility and lied again in Philadelphia, when he told his superior officer he had flying experience, when in fact he had none. In the following letters, Art explains what he did and why to his mother.

In the summer of 1918, United States was in the middle of a massive military build-up after joining WWI in April of 1917. As fate would have it, the Spanish Influenza was spreading throughout the world like a raging wildfire a mere two months before Art enlisted. From its start in Funston, Kansas in 1918 to every military camp in the US East Coast, the Spanish Influenza eventually devastated every country around the world for the next two years.

To provide context to Art's references to the influenza in his letters, the virus hit Great Lakes in late August/early September, 1918, just before he was transferred to the Philadelphia Naval Yards. In July of 1918, Great Lakes was overflowing with recruits, which is why Art's letters were written on YMCA stationary three weeks into his basic training.

Letters Home from a WWI Seaplane Test Mechanic

The letters throughout this book were originally handwritten and faithfully typed up by Helen Ehrke in 1978. My aunts Dell (Ehrke) Hummert and Lillian (Ehrke) Bostrom verified my mother's accuracy. Whenever possible, the original letterhead is included with the actual letter.

In the picture on the opposite page, the men sitting bumper to bumper eating corn on the cob in the summer of 1918 at the Great Lakes Training Station never knew that a pandemic was about to hit them just before they went to war. Art was already three weeks into his basic training when he wrote the following first letter home.

**ARMY AND NAVY
YOUNG MEN'S CHRISTIAN ASSOCIATION
"WITH THE COLORS"**

July 23, 1918

Dear Mother,

I had a few minutes and thought I would write a few letters. I didn't get a letter for about three weeks now. You didn't forget who I am or lose the address did you? Well, I ain't gone yet—and I didn't hear anything about leaving either.

I went to Chicago last Sunday and stayed at Murutske's. I had a pretty good time all right. Fred was along, and he took the machine out Sunday. I was driving, and we rode from 1:30 in the afternoon to 10 o'clock at night. We were practically all over Chicago. We were through all the different parks and Otto took us to the Chicago Auto Club, and we went to Hynlines place and to Indiana and the town of Argo. Otto thought you were coming Sunday, but you didn't. I suppose it was a little too far for you, wasn't it?

I'm certainly coming along fine. I weigh exactly 159 pounds now stripped. That's pretty good, eh? Fred is out of the hospital now and back in school. You know when I enlisted, I told them I was a Supervisor in a lathe department for a year, and I think before I get out of here, I'll be Instructor in the lathe department because the Head Instructor came and asked me what different

GREAT LAKES TRAINING STATION IN 1918

Great Lakes Training Station in the summer of 1918.
(NH 2601—Courtesy of the Naval History and Heritage Command)

Navy recruits showing off their smallpox vaccinations at the Great Lakes Training Station in 1918.
(NH53022—Courtesy of the Naval History and Heritage Command)

Letters Home from a WWI Seaplane Test Mechanic

lathes I supervised, and he took my name and Company. And I suppose as soon as I get into the machine shop, he will make me Instructor—but I don't want the job. And I'm going to try and get out of it if I can. I don't want no job like that. I could just as well stayed home if I wanted to do that kind of work.

Say, Della didn't send that money order yet did she? If she did, I didn't get it. I was figuring on coming home Saturday, but if I don't get it, I can't come. I'm pretty sure of getting paid the 5th or 20th—so after that it will be all right. It only cost me 88c to go to Otto's place and back, and I didn't have much more. And he wouldn't let me spend any money anyway.

Well, I suppose we will pass in review tomorrow—that's Wednesday afternoon, and after that I'll scrub clothes. Say, if you can get a pen for my fountain pen, get one will you? Mine is broken—they only cost about 2c, but I can't get any here. And if you get one, have it ready before Saturday—because I won't have much chance of getting any Saturday night. Otherwise, things are moving along all right.

Only thing that's worrying me is that the War might be over before I get to see anything of it, and I certainly don't want to come home from the Great Lakes. Well, that's all I know now, but don't forget to write once a month anyway. Surely with so much time you can find in a month. Well, here's hoping I get to France soon.

Your Son,

Arthur Ehrke
Company C
15th Rkg.
New Aviation Camp

TO THE WRITER: Save by writing on BOTH sides of the PAPER.

TO THE FOLKS AT HOME: Save food, BUY LIBERTY BONDS, and WAR SAVINGS STAMPS.

GREAT LAKES TRAINING STATION IN 1918

**ARMY AND NAVY
YOUNG MEN'S CHRISTIAN ASSOCIATION
"WITH THE COLORS"**

August 2, 1918

Dear Mother and Father,

Just a line to let you know that I ain't coming home this Saturday. I stayed in last Saturday, but I'm on guard from 7 o'clock to 11 Sunday morning, and the fellows are charging 25c an hour to stand guard for someone else. And if I would give my guard to some fellow that was not going to shore, I would have to pay a dollar and I ain't got any to spare, so I'll stay here and stand somebody else's guard for a dollar. I'm going to take 3 guards besides my own—so I'll make $3.00 Sunday. That will help along a little anyway. And I sure will come home next Saturday. I really would like to home this Saturday but the way it is I can't—and anyway I don't want to come home broke all the time.

I know you haven't got any too much and don't send me any more—I'll get along all right, and as soon as I get paid, I'll send home just as much as I can. I've got three more weeks of school, so that is 3 more shore leaves, and I'm almost positive that we get shipped as soon as we are through school because a class finishes up every week, and they also leave every week. But I will spend these last 3 weeks at home if I can.

Fred finishes up just one week after I do, and I don't know if he will leave the same time as I do, but if he don't, I will expect to see him come to the same place I do. Unless, as I hear, they are building aviation bases all around the coast, and I might go to a different one that he does. But we can't help that, and say, if after the war is over and I can't go into a garage or machine shop and demand the wages I want, why it won't be my fault. I've worked on motors made in England, America, and France.

I'm working on a motor now which has the propeller on the cam shaft instead of on the crank shaft like the rest have. It has 12 cyl. 6" bore and 8" stroke—some bus believe me. And we also have motors with cam shaft and rocker arms above the cylinders instead of in the motor. Last week I worked on a 21-cylinder rotary motor made in France. Believe me, that's some motor. There are 21 connecting rods on one throw of the crank shaft. That very near sounds impossible—but that's just the way it is and believe me, you have to know that motor before you get through with it too.

Pen just ran dry—so I'll have to stop.

Your loving Son,

Art Ehrke
Co. C
Aviation Camp,
Great Lakes, Ill.

P.S. I ran out of paper too, notice it.

THE
LUTHERAN BROTHERHOOD
OF AMERICA
"WITH THE COLORS"

U. S. NAVAL TRAINING STATION
BROTHERHOOD BUILDING

GREAT LAKES, ILL.   August 8, 1918

Hello there:

Well, how is everybody—pretty mad I suppose? You know we've been so busy here of late that I really had no time—but anyway I didn't hear from any of you. I'm still going to school and learning more each day.

There's a big storm blowing through here now—it is just 10 minutes to 7 and it's curtaining raining. I suppose you were wondering why I didn't come home with Fred last Saturday, eh? One reason was that I had to wash clothes, and I wanted to rate some sleep—and also no jack. I bought a razor for $2.00—it's a Gillette and

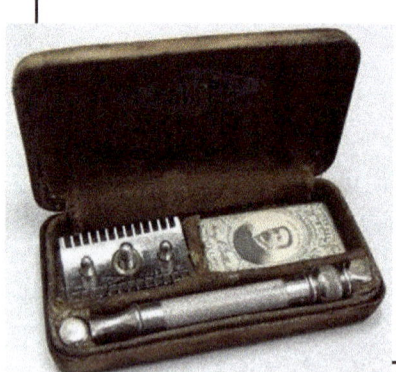

Gillette Service Razor (1918).

certainly a good one. It's a service set and the same one in town cost's $5.00.

In case you would want to come out here once more you can bring the machine right in Camp. Roads are all made, and everything is fixed up. How was the weather down there the last few days? Gee, it was warm here—about 102 degrees in the shade.

We got one of Kempsmith's millers up here—it just came in two days ago. Tomorrow the men from all over the Station are coming to the Main Camp and they are going to take a picture of the whole bunch. That will be some picture—there's about 50,000 men here—and more coming.

Notice the paper I'm using. That's from a new branch again. They have a big place in this camp, a dance hall, piano, victrola, writing room, and a stage too. Oh, it's a regular place, and when we get lots of time, we go over there—only we don't get no time.

Tell Della I'm ever so much obliged for the $1.00 she sent along with Fred. It certainly came in handy. But I expect to get paid on the 20th, and if I do, why Ill send it all back. I'm certainly having a wonderful time here. I like it better every day, and also getting heavier every day. Well, it's just about 2 and half months now that I'm gone eh? It seems about 2 and half weeks to me. The time goes so fast up here.

I see by the papers that the Dutchmen are getting beat up pretty bad. But they would get it just a little worse if Frederic-de-Ize and me were over there, and that they probably will now draft 18-45-year olds. Is that right? Well, I hope they do, so they get Louie and some of those older slackers living around there. They might get a little sense if they get in the Navy. Well, I will have to quit now for a while. I'm getting pretty sleepy.

Your son,
A. Ehrke
Company C
15th Regiment

P.S. Now don't forget to write.

Sailors assemble a Curtiss seaplane at Naval Training Center, Great Lakes, Illinois circa 1918.
(NH 2335 Curtiss Seaplane—Courtesy of Navy History and Heritage Command)

Seaplanes getting ready for a scouting mission at Great Lakes, circa 1918.
(N2497—Courtesy of the Navy History and Heritage Command)

Great Lakes Training Station in 1918

  THE
LUTHERAN BROTHERHOOD
OF AMERICA
"WITH THE COLORS"

U. S. NAVAL TRAINING STATION
BROTHERHOOD BUILDING

Great Lakes, Ill.

August 27, 1918

Dear Mother,

I had a pretty good time last Sunday night. I went to Lake Park and didn't get in until 2:30. I caught the last car at 11:45 and just before Racine, the power shut off, and we stayed there for an hour. But I was checked in at 9:45, so all's well that ends well.

That draft I was telling you about on the 27th is changed to the 15th of September, and that's the last draft leaving for France indefinitely. So I will be in it, and Fred finishes school on the 14th on Saturday, so he might go along.

And news that's going around is that we are going to a place called Poliack in France. One of the boys got a letter from there, where some of the companies are. Gee, I can't hardly wait anymore, but I suppose I'll have to.

Tomorrow is the Big Day again. Shoulder a gun and pass in review. Fred was on guard last Sunday night from 1 to 3, and he just got in fine to give the belt to the next man (lucky dog). And gee, it's fine to go to bed about 3 o'clock and get up at 5 and drill for 2 hours, work all day, and find out you are on guard the next night from 1 to 3 — just when you figure on rating a little sleep.

Oh, it's a great life. Well I'm going to bed a little early tonight so I'll have to stop.

Your loving son,

A Ehrke
Company C

Great Lakes Recruits practicing sailor's knots circa 1918.
(NH 60983NTC—Courtesy of the Naval History and Heritage Command)

Fred Eisemann and Arthur Ehrke. (family photo)

Great Lakes Training Station in 1918

THE LUTHERAN BROTHERHOOD OF AMERICA
"WITH THE COLORS"
U. S. NAVAL TRAINING STATION
BROTHERHOOD BUILDING

Great Lakes, Ill.

September 4th, 1918

Dear Mother,

Say how is it that I don't rate no mail? I didn't get any letters from home for a long time. I got new stripes put on my blouse so I won't get thrown out of line again. Well in about 2 weeks I'll come home with my first-class rating because I think I'm S.O.L. (WWI slang for "shit out of luck")

They got the list of names made out for Company C and just where they are going, and fifteen fellows that have to stay here for Instructor—and I'm one of them. Gee, I've been arguing right along to get off, but I guess there's no hope. But I'm going to try yet.

Just watch them nail Fred for Instructor in the Blacksmith Shop. I could of come in today, but it was pretty rotten out here today—raining all day long. So I thought I wouldn't come in. I'm coming in Saturday, and that will be my last time if I get off that Instructor list.

I'm in the Blacksmith Shop this week. Gee, but that's a dirty place—a fellow looks just like a coal miner when he gets home. Can you imagine me swinging a sledge all day long? That's fine dope all right.

But believe me when we hit the chow house, I sure do fill up. All hammocks washed snow-white and all lashed sea-bags all washed. Got to be hung close up against jack stove with the names on the outside and all in a line. Also floors are scrubbed and oiled and then polished. Just looks like a parlor.

Then comes the inspection and if any sea-bag has a dirty spot on it or hammocks are dirty, or the floor is dirty, why the Company loses its Liberty—and that's something nobody wants to lose. And you ought to see these guys work, and if some gob ain't working, why we holler

S.O.L. That means Save Our Liberty, and he will work then believe me.

Well I'll have to stop. We got to fall for muster in 10 minutes. But don't forget to write.

                                      A. Ehrke
                                      Company C
                                      15th Regiment
                                      Aviation Camp
                                      G.L.N.S., Ill.

P.S. I'll be home Saturday.

 **THE LUTHERAN BROTHERHOOD OF AMERICA**
"WITH THE COLORS"
U. S. NAVAL TRAINING STATION
BROTHERHOOD BUILDING

GREAT LAKES, ILL.

                                                  September 10, 1918

Dear Mother,

Well I'm rated first-class Machinist mate and I'm surely glad of it, because I told you I'd make it, and now I did. There were only six men that got first-class in our Company and I was one of them. There were eighteen that failed, and the rest made second-class. So you see you had to know a little bit to make first-class.

I'm still in Company 12 and expecting to leave any time now. Some of the men left already, and the rest are still standing by awaiting orders to shove off. The latest dope we got now is that all the first-class men from Company B and C are going to Philadelphia or to a foreign draft because they ain't sending any more second-class men over. A second-class man is only a replacement for a first-class man—and they got too many seconds over there now. So you see I'm pretty lucky.

Great Lakes Training Station in 1918

We weren't allowed to go out of our barracks this afternoon because all different orders were coming in right along, and the men weren't around to receive them. So they put two guards at each door to keep the men in. But the draft didn't come through yet, so I suppose we will get it tomorrow. There are two trains of Pullmans in the station, and I expect one is for us. I hope so anyway.

Fred finishes up Saturday and then he will know what rating he gets. He might also get a first, but you can never tell. But as long as I got it I shouldn't worry.

Say mother, I would like very much if you would send me a pair of garters, will you? Mine are torn, and I can't buy any here. Just put on Company 12, 15th Regiment, and I'll get it. I'm on guard right now and it's 9:30. I'm on from 9-11.

Last night a C.P.O. came through the barracks about 12:30 and took all the names of the men that had sticks in their hammocks, and they were restricted of liberty for a month. Can you imagine that? I didn't have any, so I was O.K. And the fellows that did have ain't worrying because they know they are going to ship out pretty soon.

Well, here's hoping to hear from you soon, and also that I go across soon.

Your loving son,
A. Ehrke
Co. 12, 15 Reg.
Aviation Camp
G.L. Ill.

Letters Home from a WWI Seaplane Test Mechanic

Family photo of Della and Arthur.

September 12, 1918

AE:

Art, Mother did not get a letter from you, but Adelle did. Now I just want to tell you a few things, and please take it a little sisterly advice—because I know and you don't. First, don't set your heart on Adelle, because she is terribly fickle. I have absolute proof that she is writing 5 or 6 soldiers, etc., all this love stuff, and is in other words—boy crazy. Mr. Wright himself said that he saw her lie around the trucks with the soldiers when here, and I wouldn't want my brother to fall in love. Now, I'm not saying you are because I don't believe it, but even as much as be on intimate terms with a girl of that sort. She isn't to be trusted any further than you can see her.

At present she is wearing rings of a dozen other fellows and crows how much this one loves her, and that one. She is all right to have a good time with once in a while, but that's enough. Stay your distance, and be careful what you write to her, because she keeps noth-

Great Lakes Training Station in 1918

ing to herself, and blabbers everything to the Zastrow girls, and in short the whole city of West Allis knows about what you wrote to her. She is only playing with you. The way she dolls up—why I was ashamed the other day on the streetcar to be seen with her—she had her lashes blackened so, and so much paint on, that everyone in the streetcar made remarks—and she didn't care a bit. Lord, a girl like that has a lot to learn. True, she has many good points too, but when it comes to loving fellows she tells everyone the selfsame story, and just wants them to send her souvenirs etc., so she can blabber over W.A. what she got.

Now remember, Art, the truest friends you have are your folks and your sisters, and believe me I'll stick to you to the last, and if any of these vampire girls want to stick their nose in your affairs, and crow about it to everybody, well I'm there to tell them where to get off at. If you want good girls you can get them—but please don't get too intimate with such girls. It doesn't pay.

Why Mrs. Wichman was telling women at the Women's Aid that Ma goes to, that Adella was writing to you and you to her, and perhaps you two would get together someday. Why ma said she didn't know what to think or say. Why didn't you write home? You had better cause you don't how much your Mother is worrying about you, and what she did Sunday Night was only for your good, and Adella was no lady, and I have nothing to do with that sort.

Art, I must close, and as this is Milwaukee Day at the States Fair I am going there this afternoon, and wish you were here to join us. Don't forget to write Mother, and anything you want to know, or have, let me know at the office, cause I'll do anything for you.

I want to send you something for your birthday, so let us know your correct address, and Art, please remember this one thing—"Steer clear from girls who love every fellow" and have no self respect. You don't know what they are, but we have some awful cases right here at the office of such girls,--and I know.

With loads of love to you. I am as ever,

Your sister Della

Note: When Arthur was transferred to Philadelphia, he kept a WWI health pamphlet named *An Appeal to Men* from a Philadelphia urologist named Doctor Cauffman. If you would like to read his articles about *Men's Follies, Lost Manhood and the Results of Secret Sin*, go to Appendix 2 at the end of the book to read more about Cauffman's advice about *Love, Courtship and Marriage*.

WWI MM1 Machinist's Mate First Class insignia.

Great Lakes Training Station in 1918

THE LUTHERAN BROTHERHOOD OF AMERICA
"WITH THE COLORS"

U. S. NAVAL TRAINING STATION
BROTHERHOOD BUILDING

Great Lakes, Ill.   September 13, 1918

Dear Mother,

Well how is everything coming along in West Allis? Say everyone listen, I've received my first-class rating and wear three stripes instead of two. There were only six men in our Company that received first—so you see I know a little bit anyway.

Well I got some more news for you—maybe you won't like it, but believe me I do. I'm in Camp Luce now—that's the outgoing detention camp and a friend in our Company knows the Chief yeoman at headquarters and we went to find out when we shove off, and this is what we found out. We are on the draft Number 474, leaving Camp Luce Monday September 16th—a day before my birthday for a receiving ship at Philadelphia and then go across.

Now what do you think of that? Sure is just the way I wanted it so I can't come home no more until we beat them over there. Now this is absolutely the way it's going.

About twenty-five of our men went for aerial gunners, and they are going to Pensacola, Florida Monday, and about twenty are held for Instructors, and the rest are with us. So then I'll spend the Winter across, and I'm going to take it all in too, believe me.

In the barracks we are now in, there are only twenty-five men, and we eat and sleep in it too. I'm on the mess detail for this Company and we rate the best of grub now we are leaving. We had spaghetti, potato salad, pork chops, pickles, pears, wheat bread, butter, jam and coffee.

I've got to hit the deck, excuse haste.

                                    Your loving son,

                                              A. Ehrke
                                         Co. 28, 17 Reg.
                                      Camp Luce, G.L. Ill.

THE LUTHERAN BROTHERHOOD OF AMERICA
"WITH THE COLORS"
U. S. NAVAL TRAINING STATION
BROTHERHOOD BUILDING

GREAT LAKES, ILL.

September 17, 1918

Dear Mother:

I'm still at Camp Luce but I haven't received any mail for about two weeks. Most all camps are quarantined now, and all the sick bays are filled. I ain't sick yet, and don't think I will either. I was supposed to be on my way now, but all the Eastern camps are quarantined, so I can't leave yet. Newport in Virginia is the only camp that ain't quarantined, but the aviator bunch don't go there. Part of or Company has gone to Pensacola, Florida. They were aerial gunners. I could have been an aerial gunner, but I didn't like it.

We are wearing our blues—that's the uniform of the day from last Monday on all through winter. It's pretty cold up here. We are only a half a block from the lake. We all got another comfort kit from the Navy Relief Service today. There was a comb, toothbrush, buttons, soap, thread, clothes stops, needles, and safety pins, and a bag. Everyone gets them before he leaves the station.

It's certainly rotten in this camp now that all the other camps quarantined. A fellow can't get a haircut or even buy any tobacco, and I'm sure in need of that.

Say, what do you know about it--today is my birthday and I never thought of it at all. Well that is another year gone. Next year at this time I might be flying somewhere in France, eh?

How is everyone feeling down home? Did any of you get sick? Gee you ought to see how it is up here—most everyone is sick. There were twelve that died between aviation camp and main camp.

I wrote to Harvey some time ago but he didn't answer. I don't know if he got it or not, but maybe he is busy working I suppose and he ain't got no time.

Great Lakes Training Station in 1918

How was State Fair this year—same as always? I know I didn't miss much there anyway. Only I wish the old influenza was over so we would shove off. Us mess cooks certainly have it soft up here. All we have to do is swab the floor, wash dishes, and clean up the kitchen, and also serve the chow. That takes about two and a half hours. Then we can do anything we want until 11:30 and the same thing in the afternoon. The mess cooks don't rate no guard duty and no detail work and don't have to answer muster. The rest of the boys have to guard at night and do detail work all day. Believe me I know a snap when I see one. I'll have to close now, with best wishes.

> Your loving Son,
> Arthur Ehrke
> Co.28, 17th Reg.
> Camp Luce
> G.L. Ill.

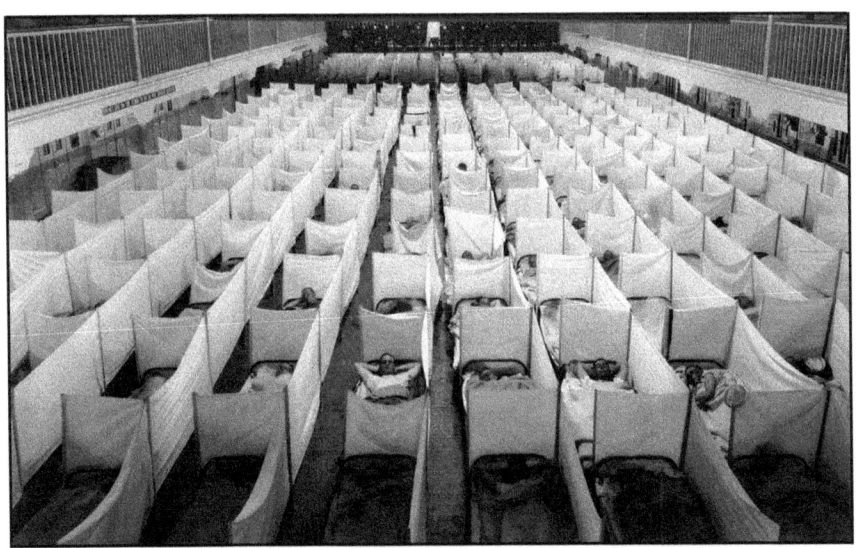

During the 1918 pandemic, the Navy erected "sneeze guards" around beds to curb transmission. (NH 41871—Courtesy of the Naval History and Heritage Command)

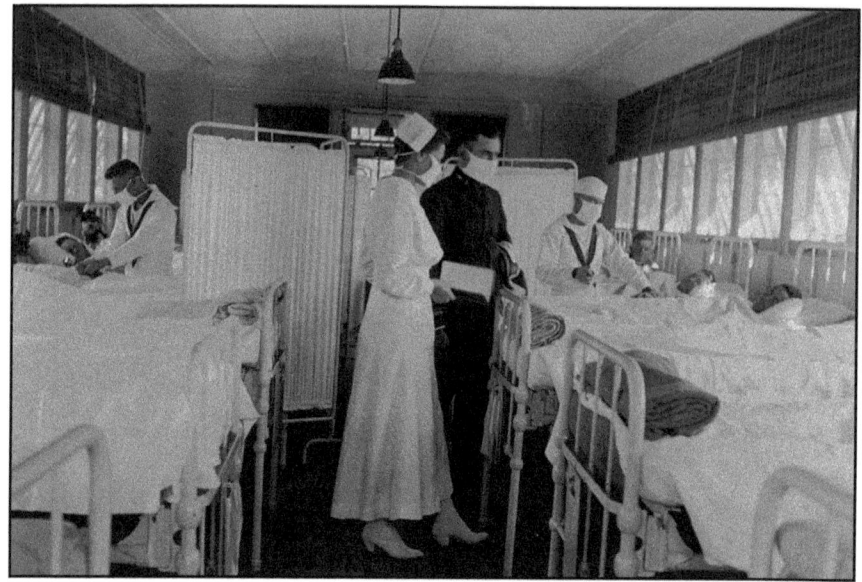

Naval hospital in Gulfport, Miss. during the 1918 pandemic.
(H-022-1—Courtesy of the Naval History and Heritage Command)

Crowded WWI U.S. troop ship on its way to Europe,
which became an unwitting vector for disease transmission.
(Courtesy of the Naval History and Heritage Command)

Chapter Three
The Spanish Influenza and Philadelphia's Naval Aircraft Factory

The Navy's seaplane float in Philadelphia's 1918 Fourth Liberty Loan Parade.
(NH 41730—Courtesy of the Naval History and Heritage Command)

Art left on a train headed to the East Coast on Wednesday morning, September 18th, one day before Great Lakes cancelled all liberties and quarantined the whole base. September 18th also happened to be day the Spanish Influenza hit the sprawling Naval Yards, which included the newly minted Navy

Airplane Factory built in Philadelphia the previous year. Sadly, the next day, 600 sailors became ill and local hospitals immediately filled up.

Due to the war effort, Philadelphia's population had recently swelled to two million. With housing units filled to the brim, the City of Brotherly Love was about to become the epicenter of the Spanish Influenza in United States. On September 28th, 1918, one of many WWI super-spreader events occurred, when two hundred thousand people gathered within 23 blocks to view the kickoff of the Fourth Liberty Loan Drive in Philadelphia.

By October 4th, a devastating surge of deaths began. Philadelphia's Board of Health immediately suggested people refrain from coughing, sneezing or spitting. Officials shut down every school,

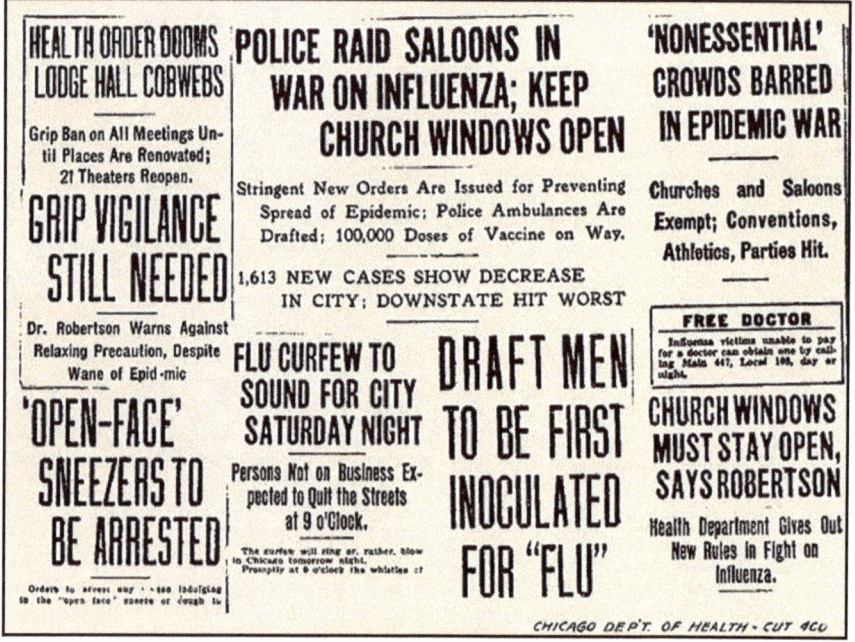

Mitigation Strategies from 1918 Chicago newspaper headlines, which included useless inoculations, increased ventilation, arrests for not wearing face masks, crowd limitations, selective business closings, curfews, and lockdowns. (Chicago Dept. of Health)[2]

---

[1] Lynch, E. "The Flu of 1918." *The Pennsylvania Gazette*, University of Pennsylvania, 17 February 1999.

[2] "We're celebrating Thanksgiving amid a pandemic. Here's what we did in 1918—what happened next." *USA Today*. Archived from the original on 21 November 2020.

church, theater and saloon. Gauze masks were required in public with the warning, *"Obey the laws and wear the gauze...protect your jaws from septic paws."*[1] Those who refused to wear masks were called "slackers," which meant something to a patriotic citizenry at war a century ago. Occasionally, slackers were run off the streets and coughs would send people scurrying.

Initially, Chicago's strict containment measures were successful by some measures by the end of October 1918. But the Armistice Day celebrations in November and relaxed Thanksgiving restrictions caused a resurgence. Since Prohibition was about to become law around the country, people ran to pharmacies to fill their prescriptions for whiskey, which was the only place to get useless flu remedies and alcohol for medicinal purposes.

After the Fourth Liberty Loan Parade in Philadelphia, every hospital within the city was overflowing with the sick and dying. Nurses destined for the Front in France stayed home to attend to the crisis. The annual report of Philadelphia's Chestnut Hill Hospital's

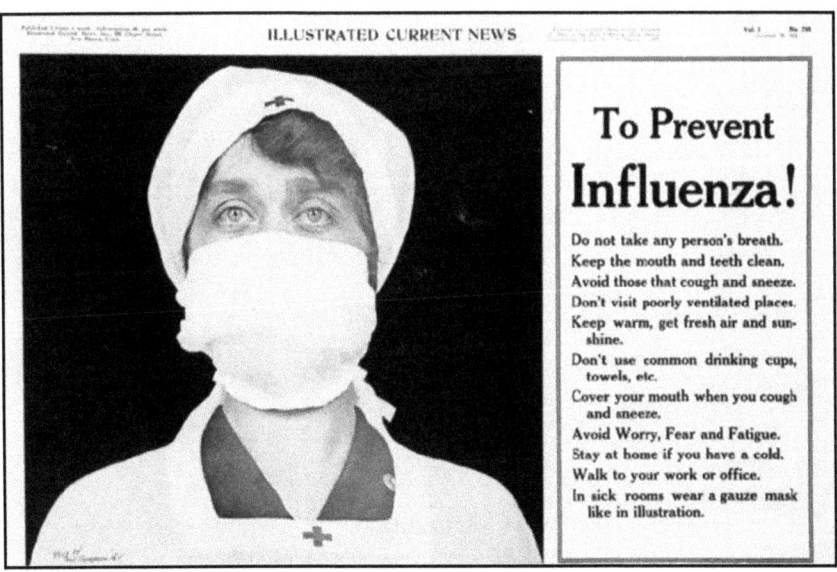

Public health recommendations from the 1918 *Illustrated News*, New Haven, CT.

---

[3] Chestnut Hill Hospital School of Nursing, *Annual Report*, 1918.

School of Nursing described the pandemic as "most tragic because of the loss by death of so many nurses and because of our inability to meet the needs of patients who came to us during the epidemic of influenza that swept the city."[3]

To offer perspective, visiting nurses were the first to enter homes when the whole family had recently perished. When parents died, children starved and countless needed shelters. Some neighborhoods hailed the visiting nurses as heroes and other's shunned them because they wore masks.[4] Some brave souls helped their neighbors and others, fearful of contracting the disease, refused. Bodies quickly overwhelmed hospital morgues and the deceased lay on street corners. Not since the Black Death in medieval Europe did carts roam the streets as they did in Philadelphia, calling for those still living to bring out their dead. Highway workers dug large trenches to bury the dead in mass graves. The city promised loved ones that they could retrieve their relatives later, but only a few family members took them up on their offer.

Ambulance in front of the Girls Club of Philadelphia during the pandemic.
(Courtesy of the National Archives and Records Administration)

---

[4] Philadelphia Society of Visiting Nurses, *Annual Report*, 1918.

The Spanish Influenza / Philadelphia's Naval Aircraft Factory

A trainload of sailors shipping out of Great Lakes circa 1918.
(NH 2483—Courtesy of the Naval History and Heritage Command)

By October 27th, 1918, the epidemic started to subside in Philadelphia. In just four weeks 47,094 people contracted the influenza and 12,191 people had perished. Art talked about the pandemic in his letters and worried about his family, but never contracted the disease. Art's letters continue when he arrived in Philadelphia just before the Fourth of July Liberty Loan parade after he shipped out and enjoyed the comforts of the Red Cross volunteers at the train stations along the way.

```
                                                    Philadelphia
                                               September 21, 1918
Dear Mother:

Well I'm here now, and I sure had one nice trip. We left
Great Lakes Wednesday morning at 6:30 and went to
Chicago. Stayed there an hour and 35 minutes, then got
in our Pullman and rode all day. Went through Chicago,
Indiana, Ohio, Pittsburgh and up to Washington. We got
to Washington at 10:30 Thursday morning. We stayed there
until 1 o'clock. I saw the Capitol and all kinds of
government buildings.
```

Red Cross workers at Union Station, Savannah, GA.
(Courtesy of the Georgia Historical Society)

Gee, it sure was great all along these Stations were Red Cross women giving us apples, sandwiches, doughnuts, cigarettes and candy. From Washington we went to Baltimore and that's another good place. We are right on the Delaware Bay-just a stone's throw from there.

I'm expecting to go across any day now. I hope they shake it up a little. I saw the Belgium Relief Ship come in today. Just came from France. It had Belgium Relief painted clean across the sides. You ought to of seen the big mountains coming through Ohio and Pennsylvania. All stone, and the railroad runs through some of them. They got little electric cars pulling the whole train through the tunnels. I slept in the lower berth on the Pullman and it sure was fine sleeping. We ate in the diner—had ham and eggs and all kinds of dope. Everything was good. I'll have to stop now as I am in a hurry. We're sleeping in tents again, but we will only be here a short while.

Philadelphia is sure a nice town. We get liberty every night from 5:30 to 7:30 the next morning, and from noon Saturday until 7:30 Monday morning. I didn't get paid either. We left just before payday and now we have to wait until next month. They ain't got anything to sleep on here, and when we got here just about 5 o'clock—all dirty, they told us to go to town and sleep at the YMCA.

The Spanish Influenza / Philadelphia's Naval Aircraft Factory

```
So we had to go—it only cost 5c to go to town and 35c
for a bed. That was just about as much as I had. After
we get across they only pay us $7.00 a month and save
the rest for us.

Well, I'll write you later,
                                    Your loving son,
                                       A. Ehrke
                                    Co. I Camp Sims
                                       Navy Yards
                                 Philadelphia, Penn.
```

```
                                   September 24, 1918

Hello everybody,

It's just 15 minutes to 6 now and just finished Supper.
I've got six pieces of gingerbread here so I won't
starve while I'm writing. I didn't receive any mail for
about two weeks. I was just wondering if you wrote or
not. I'm still at this tent city but expect to move
shortly.
```

Philadelphia's thirty-one hospitals were filled to capacity within seventy-two hours after the September 30th, 1918, Liberty Loan Parade.
(ARC ID 45491853—Courtesy of the National Archives at College Park)

How is everything coming along at home? Did any of you catch the Spanish Influenza? Gee, it' something awful here. The hospital wagon keeps taking jacks to sickbay every little while. There were twenty-five that died since I came here-so you can imagine how it is. I'm pretty lucky so far. I ain't been in the sickbay since I joined the Navy-and I don't figure I will either. We got a lot of Negroes and Filipinos up here. The spikes are little fellows-only about 5 feet high, all got black hair and dark tan skin, they run around here like flies. Uncle Sam uses them for mess hall work. They're the cleanest people you have ever seen.

Just a minute till I load my pipe-all set, let's go. I just 900 miles from home now, and still going farther once I get across. I don't care when the war ends, but I'm hoping it won't till I do get there. It sure is great up here-you sit here evenings and watch the boats go by. All of them are camouflaged all colors of the rainbow-but most are painted gray-black and white, and when you see it a mile off-you can't tell what it is, how big, or which is the front or rear end.

I was working yesterday. I was on the ship Pensacola and was heaving coal from the reserve bunker to the boiler room bunker-a great job. But when chow call blew,

USS Pensacola.
(NH 50186—Courtesy of Naval History and Heritage Command)

The Spanish Influenza / Philadelphia's Naval Aircraft Factory

believe me, I felt like eating and did too. I didn't do anything today. I was swimming in Delaware Bay all morning. And this afternoon, I was laying on the beach watching them test seaplanes. They are anchored in the water all along the river, and there's every kind imaginable. They are building a lot of bombing planes with two liberty motors on them. The machine only weighs 12,000 pounds. Can you imagine a big thing like that going in the air, but they do go, and they are building the pusher type with the propeller between the tail and wings. They got two sets of wings on these planes-something they ain't got on the others. And they got these little scout planes with two pontoons-them are some speedy devils. You only have to go about 300 feet in the water and she will rise. These big ones have to go about five or six blocks before they rise.

There are three warships here in the channel and two submarines. This is a regular Navy Yard this is. Just across the river from where I am-is New Jersey and the DuPont powder works. If I stay here long enough I'm going to see New York. It's only 91 miles from here but I don't think I'll be here long. Part of Company is gone already. There is a draft courier in every morning in every morning and I might be sent out any day. There is still one man left of old Company 190 with me.

(The rest of the letter is missing)

DuPont Powder Works from a 1907 postcard.
The Hagley Museum is located on the site of the gunpowder works founded by E.I. DuPont in 1802. (Courtesy of the Hagley Museum and Library)

12-cylinder Liberty motor, Naval Aviation Factory, Philadelphia 1918.
(NH 44106—Courtesy of the Naval History and Heritage Command)

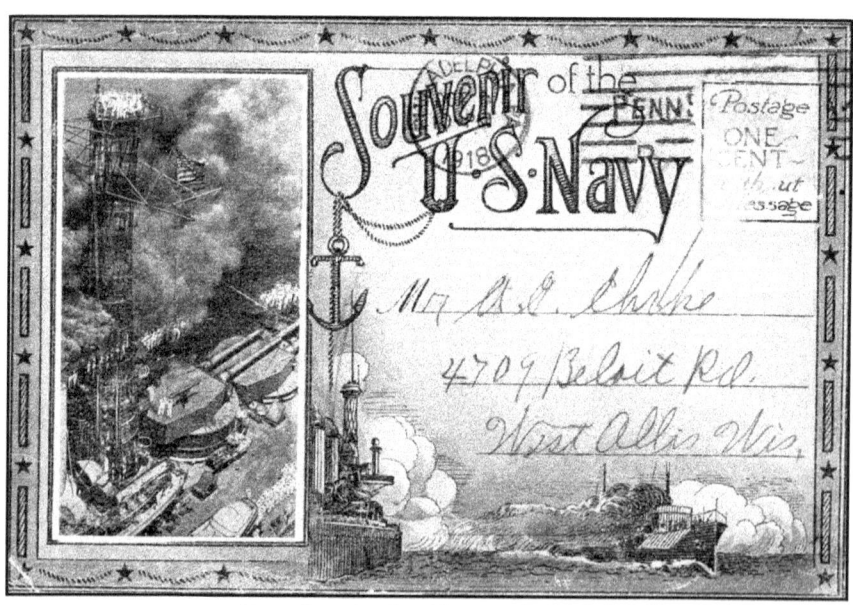

Souvenir postcard sent home to the family.

The Spanish Influenza / Philadelphia's Naval Aircraft Factory

October 6, 1918

Dear Folks,

I am now at the YMCA in the City of Philadelphia. How are all the Folks—any sick yet? I hope not. I'm just as well as always. I weigh 168 pounds now and feel like a lark. I haven't heard from Fred or Harvey either, but suppose they are pretty busy.

Did you hear of the Battleship Minnesota being torpedoed? Maybe you didn't hear about it, but I've seen it. She is in dry-dock now, and there's a hole in her about 40 feet long, 20 feet high and almost clean through it. The armor plate on her was torn as if it was paper. She was making 15 knots when hit, and she just barely crawled in port with three destroyers as escorts. Also South Carolina had one of her propellers shot off. You might not hear about this in the newspapers, but I've seen it.

I'm in a new Company again and expect to cross the pond anytime now. I got paid the 4th, and drew $56.00—also bought a Liberty Bond. They take 17c of my money every day to pay for it. I figured on sending some home, but Mother if I go across we only get $7.00 a month, and the

USS Minnesota at the Philadelphia Navy Yard.
(NH 61215—Courtesy of the Naval History and Heritage Command)

rest is saved for us. So I will need a little money yet, but if I don't need it all, I'll send it home or else pay it on my Bond and send that home.

You know we had bag inspection Friday and we have to draw more clothes, and expect to draw them Monday. We have to have three pairs of shoes, also six suits of summer and winter underwear and things like that. The whole works will amount to about $40.00 before we are fully equipped, and you have to be fully equipped before you go across. And I also have to buy stationary, tooth paste, shaving soap, face soap, washing soap, shoe-strings, and all little things like that. I've got to buy another grip-mine is on the hooks. All little things like that count up and I don't want to go across and be wanting this and that and then can't get it. So if I don't send any money home just now, don't think that I'm spending it and having a good time because I ain't. And I couldn't if I wanted to because all the theaters, cafes, and clubs are closed on account of this sickness. But as soon as I get my Bond, or if I have money I don't need, I'll send it to you.

I haven't received the box yet, but I suppose it's on the way. Philadelphia is a pretty nice town. Sailors and Soldiers are admitted free into all theaters—all they have to pay is the war-tax. But they are all closed now,

WHEN THE FLU HIT THE AIRCRAFT BUNCH

When your back is broke and your eyes are blurred
And your shin bones knock and your tongue is flurred
And your tonsils squeak and your hair gets dry,
And your doggone sure you're going to die,
But you're skeered you won't and afraid you will,
Just drag to bed and have your chill,
And pray the Lord to see you through,
For you've got the Flu, Boy,
        You've got the Flu.

From the *Logbook of the Naval Aircraft Association 1917-1918*.

> and there's nothing to do. I left the Yards at 12 o'clock last night with two of the boys and we took a walk in the country.
>
> This morning I wish you were here to see some of the shipyards at Hog Island. They are turning out ships everyday. That's the biggest shipyard in the U.S. Well, I'll have to close. I'm going to dinner.
>
> Your loving Son,
A. Ehrke
Barracks 260
League Island Navy Yards
>
> P.S. Now write once in a while anyway.

A Fleet at the End of a Fleeting Year

The picture above and the following information about the birth of the Naval Aircraft Factory come from the facility's *Naval Logbook 1917-1918*. Art's letters continue afterwards.

NAVAL AIRCRAFT ASSOCIATION

"In the Beginning . . . . . the Earth was without Form"

THE PLANT THAT GREW UP

"SCIENTIFIC AMERICAN" CALLS NAVY YARD AIRCRAFT PLANT A WONDER

ON THE 27th of July, 1917, Secretary of the Navy Daniels affixed his signature to a document, which authorized the construction of the only Government-owned aircraft factory this country has ever possessed. This date marks the birth of the Naval Aircraft Factory; fourteen days later at the League Island Navy Yard, in Philadelphia, construction work itself actually began. It was truly a pioneer undertaking and like all such undertakings the very breadth of its possibilities was measured also by the difficulties attendant upon its construction.

One of its slogans from the very beginning was speed, and still more speed. From the day the first spade struck earth the work proceeded with an incredible swiftness. On the 16th of October the first machinery started in motion; three weeks later the keel of the first boat seaplane was laid, and in March, 1918, the first service machine produced by the factory successfully accomplished its initial flight.

The original manufacturing unit with a ground area of 160,000 square feet is a permanent steel structure of the most durable type. It was built and equipped in about three months' time at a cost of a million dollars; and the mechanics followed so closely on the heels of the builder that the entire plant was in operation before the building was completed.

Early in January, 1918, the Navy's aircraft program was very largely expended, carrying it far beyond the manufacturing facilities hitherto assigned to the Navy. Quite naturally this brought about an enlargement of the factory, comprising five buildings with a floor area five times that of the original plant. The augmented program required new aircraft faster than they could be provided by building an entirely balanced factory. The authorities therefore contemplated that the new extension should be an assembly plant and in proportion to its growth, privately-owned manufacturing facilities be taken off their regular commercial work and placed under contract to furnish the hulls, wings and other parts needed. Thus branches of this establishment appeared in many places through the East and turned their activities to a common end under the direction of the Naval Aircraft Factory's staff of engineers.

The new plant was designed with generous dimensions for the accommodation of such larger sizes of planes as the future might develop; and the plant itself was laid out for manufacture on modern lines, presenting particularly the feature of progressive assembly.

A glimpse of the buildings which now extend over forty acres of ground along the Delaware offers visual proof of the completeness with which the whole undertaking was accomplished. One broadside view of the assembly plant gives the onlooker the impression of a huge reflector; with its thousands of square feet of almost solid glass, the effect is truly striking. Within the building, the impression is intensified; the long busy place is literally bathed in sunlight and humming with activity. On one side is seen a tremendous hull, swung overhead by a traveling crane; on another, completed wing panels assembled for inspection, each set spreading over a hundred feet in length; ahead is a department where women in overalls are contributing their share of work to the finished whole.

Beyond, a train pulls out of the factory with planes packed for shipment overseas. In truth, the manufacturing unit of this aircraft factory is several industries in one. There is a large wood-working division, a complete metal shop, and a boatbuilding plant, each with numerous subdivisions. And then there is the huge assembly division which assembles parts supplied by outside plants, as already mentioned.

Plant 1, Office, Stores, and Plant 2

When a manager was selected, the site of the Naval Aircraft Factory was a level bit of pasture. Few men have been assigned a task that loomed so large from the very beginning. In this instance the expression, "Built from the ground up," applied to the very letter. To Naval Constructor F. G. Coburn was assigned the management of the enterprise, and because of his wide experience as a naval architect and marine engineer, as well as considerable industrial experience, it would be difficult indeed to find a man better qualified for the post.

Obviously, the first step was the securing of an executive force as a nucleus, and as the officers of the regular Navy were needed elsewhere, the manager went about selecting from civil life men peculiarly adapted to the needs of such an undertaking. It is interesting to note that no two of the principal department heads came from the same line of industry.

A feature of the process of developing personnel is the apprenticeship school for women. From all walks of life have come women with no previous training and actuated only by patriotism and the needs of the times. Most of their work from the start is on the actual product, thus no time, labor or interest is lost. They are carefully instructed in factory methods and rules. The effectiveness of the means used in adding women to the factory's personnel may well be expressed in figures, since nearly 1,000 of the 3,600 employes are women and their work is a factor in practically every department.

Like all sagacious employers of today, the Naval Aircraft Factory takes good care of its workers. Light, air, heat, pleasant surroundings—all these factors enter into keeping the personnel at the highest pitch of enthusiasm and efficiency. A cafeteria, far above the average, is operated within the factory and three meals a day are here obtainable. During the noonday luncheon period a Naval band furnishes relaxation.

End view at year's end

Down below 3,000 feet—all there

At first glance the giant seaplane of our Navy appears formidable while resting on the water, and still more so when hauled up on shore where its boat-like body lies fully uncovered to view. In flight it does not seem so large; indeed, it might well be mistaken for the smaller flying boats by the layman, since all aircraft are deceptive while in flight. But viewed close up there can be no mistake about the size of this craft, with its 110-foot span, two Liberty motors developing from 400 to 500 horsepower each and driving propellers 10½ feet in diameter, and a body over 50 feet in length. The fact is that the body, or hull, is nothing short of a 50-foot yacht, but instead of velvet-cushioned berths and other comforts, its interior is given over to a tangle of braces, wires, steering and controlling devices, instruments, a wireless station, a six-station intercommunicating telephone system, fuel tanks and guns, all of which are the means of combating the U-boat and of carrying out long-distance patrols at sea. On the water the seaplane develops a speed up to fifty miles an hour, and the moment it slips off the surface and soars upwards the speed increases to 100 miles an hour.

When Arthur went in to work in the Navy Yards, the following message greeted him.

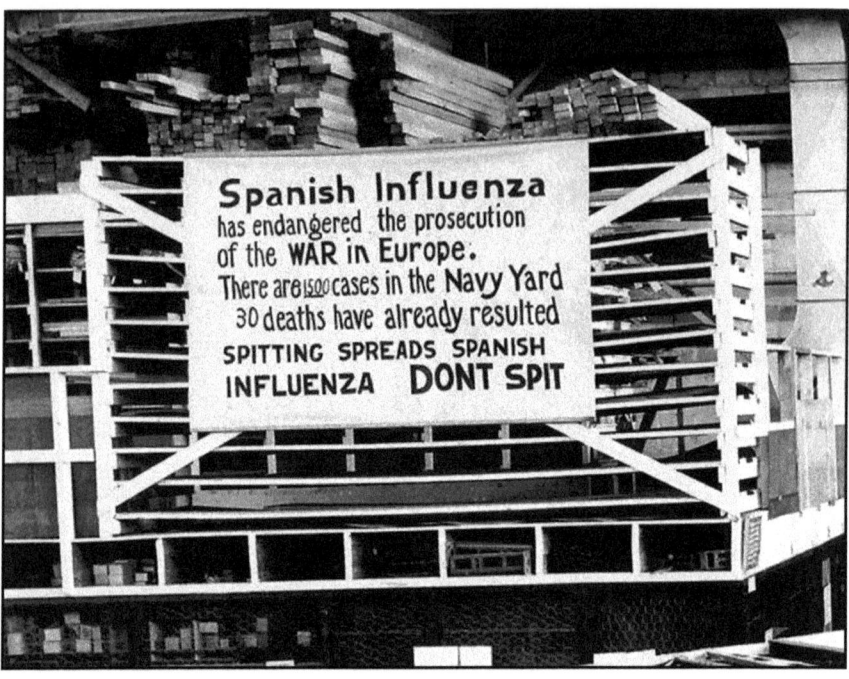

Sign at a Naval Aircraft factory in Philadelphia, Oct. 19. 1918.
(NH 41731—Courtesy of the Naval History and Heritage Command)

```
                                            October 21, 1918
Hello Folks,

Just finished chow and thought I would write a few lines
to let you know how everything is coming along in Phila-
delphia. From the first of the month (Nov.1) I'm going
to be put on subsistence and receive $90.00 per month
for board and room besides my $66.50, which I will re-
ceive for my work. That will be $156.50 per month--$6.50
for insurance, $5.09 for Bond, and 20c for hospital
dues.

Now what do you think of Mickey?

I've got a friend up here, who lives in New Jersey and I
can get my board and room pretty reasonable in his home,
```

Advertisement in *Moving Picture World* for the film Mickey (1918)

Mickey was the highest-grossing silent film in 1918. Mickey, the character, was a free-spirited, uncultured adult orphan, who eventually becomes happy in love, her marriage, and very wealthy.

and as soon as I get settled a little, I'll send money home every month. I sure like this work, and learning more every day. I expect to make my first flight some day this week. We are supposed to make at least one flight a week. That's government orders you see. We don't pilot the machine but we have to watch the motors and all the gasoline and oil gauges.

Three of our machines started on a flight of 2,300 miles at 7 o'clock this morning. They are bound to Pensacola, Florida. That's some trip. Twelve men from the hanger were with them, and if I would have been working here for about a month, I could of gone along. But they will fly some more over there in a short while, and my chance is next. We have just twenty-five Sailors working here, and they change of making trips like that. We had to work Saturday afternoon, most of the night, and all day Sunday getting these planes ready for this trip. We had to go over every part of the plane and test all the wires, we had to put on two sea anchors, hose clamps, extra propellers, carburetors, and pistols. These are 10 gauge pistols, which shot red, white, green, and blue flames for signals. It took all day Sunday to tune up the motors. These machines carry 285 gallons of gasoline and 13 gallons of oil-but each motor uses one gallon of gas every minute so that gas don't last long.

How would you like to buy gasoline for a trip like that? But Uncle Sam has got lots of money-so we shouldn't worry. It rained last Sunday and there was an awful storm and you can imagine us going out to these machines-testing motors, filling tanks, and all this and that. Believe me, it ain't no snap. And everything has got to be done fast, but I don't mind working hard on something I like to work at. Trying to anchor these machines in a storm just returning from a flight is some job and I fell in the river trying to do this same thing on Sunday. But I got out all right and all's well.

I sure wish Fred would come up here. I would try and get him in here. I know he would like it. It's pretty hard to get in here if you don't know anybody working here. It took me just one month of chewing the rag to get myself where I am. But I am here now and I want to make Chief before I get out of here, and if I try hard enough, I don't see why I can't. I'm going to show all my Aunts and Uncles just what kind of stuff I'm made of. I hear Harvey is Corporal-but it don't take much brains to be Corporal of truck drivers.

I told everyone I was going to make first-class-and I done it, and now I'm telling you that I'll make Chief

Adelia, Lillian, and Walter Ehrke in the Grant with Mom looking on through the window.

before Spring now—just see if I don't make it. I heard Louie is in the Army Aviation—well I wish him all the luck in the world, but I think the war will be over before he gets started.

Say, how is the Grant? Still running I suppose? I wouldn't mind taking a little spin right now, but I suppose I'll have to wait a little while yet.

They are building a transatlantic seaplane up in these factories—that's a plane built to fly across the ocean. I ain't supposed to say anything about it, but I'll tell you a little bit about it anyway. They have five Liberty motors on this one and it carries enough gasoline to carry it across. Also fifteen mechanics and three pilots, and I sure hope to get this one for a test. It ain't finished yet, but will be in about a month.

I'll have to close now, as I want to wash a few hats before I retire.

Your loving son,
Arthur E. Ehrke
League Island, N.Y.
Philadelphia, Pa.
Aviation barracks 263

P.S. My pictures ought to be there Thursday morning.

October 24, 1918

Dear Mother,

Received your letter and the gist of it is that I'm getting balled out, is that right? Well, I'm used to that. You say Uncle Henry sent me a box about two weeks ago? I never received so such box as yet, and I don't know his address, so I can't write him.

Also you would like to know why I don't use YMCA stationary. Well there are two reasons. For the first one is—that this is a Navy Yard and no training station, and the second is that the only place where we could possibly get it is closed on account of the Flu. So you see, I'm out of luck and have to buy it.

Letters Home from a WWI Seaplane Test Mechanic

Curtiss C-1 Bomber.
(Courtesy of the City of Toronto Archives, listed under the archival citation Fonds 1244, Item 4519)

But listen to this and see how it sounds. I'm on a flying crew now on a bombing plane C-1 and expect to fly to Pensacola with it about Wednesday morning. That's 2,300 miles from here. The other three machines arrived there yesterday and didn't have any trouble. Now what do you think of that? My job on this trip will be to watch the gasoline valves, gauges, oil gauges and water gauges, and I have to make a report in a log of just how these gauges act every hour while flying. And of course, all five of us have to take care of the motors. Each man has his duties to perform on a trip like this and each one is important of course. None of us pilots the machine—a lieutenant does that-but we have more responsibility than he has because if our part doesn't work right, his surely won't. Now that's what I call real life, and everyone in West Allis said I would never have a chance to fly!

Watch me, and I'll show them all. I wouldn't of got on this crew if I didn't use a little strategy. All the other men on this crew have been up before, and they asked me if I was ever up before. Why, of course I was, I told them. I was up on land planes, so that's how I got this royal flying crew.

Seaplane view of Naval Air Station, Hampton Roads.
United States Bureau of Yards and Docks, Navy Department World War 1917-1918.
(Courtesy of the Hampton Roads Naval Museum)

You know I ain't asleep when something like this is pulled up. We will make two stops on the trip-one at Hampton Roads, and one at Charleston in South Carolina, and I'll write from each stop as we get there. The flying time is thirty-eight hours. It will take about three days to get there if everything works right, and then come back on the train. So if we go on Wednesday, I don't expect to return for about a week and a half considering it comes out as planned.

And when I come back from there, nobody will be able to talk to me. I got a letter from Fred today and he says that he is coming up here. I sure wish he would, because he will surely like it here. I'm going to bed now, so I'll have to quit.

Your son,
A. Ehrke
League Island Navy Yard
Philadelphia, Pa.
Aviation Barracks 263

Lillian Ehrke, Fred Eisemann, Arthur and an unknown friend.

```
                                              Oct. 31, 1918
Dear Folks,

Well I met my old buddy Fred, and he came up here about
two days ago and I'm going to try and get him in the
hanger if I can, so we can both room together. I took
him out last night and showed him a little of the town
and we are going to Fairmount Park this afternoon. That
trip to Florida I was telling you about is off for a
while because our Pilot has got the flu.

I've had two trips in the air so far—about two hours in
the air altogether. I was Observer on the first trip and
it sure is great stuff. We went up in the rain, and be-
lieve me that stuff sure cuts. We were up two thousand
feet and the river looked like a small creek. And we
struck air pockets in the air—and you can't imagine how
that feels. It's just like riding a Grant on a rough
road—that's just the way it seems.
```

I was hanging out from my waistline and the wind goes in your clothes, and everything feels like rubber, and the wind blows your cheeks in between your teeth, and that you feel funny the first time you go up-but they don't know what they're talking about. It's just the same as riding a car-only you go up and come down.

Fred saw me go up the second time and he sure would of liked to go up too, but if he gets in here his chance will come.

How is everything in West Allis? Are you quarantined yet? Philadelphia just opened up October 30th. Say Fred was telling me that Pa wants to take the car apart. Well that would be a good idea, but watch your step. You can't imagine all the things you have to watch with an ignition system like you got, because we got a Delco system on the Liberties, and they work on the same principle. And I've taken enough apart to know if you do take it apart, center punch your timing gears and watch how your spark is set. You wouldn't have to mark these parts if you knew how to adjust them again.

Why don't you wait a little? That War won't last long, and we can both take it down.

Fairmount Park souvenir postcard from 1918.

Say, Fred only got a second-class rating. He told his folks he got a first, but he said he didn't get it. Now don't tell his folks about it, because he would only hear it again.

Well, I'm closing now, as I have a few more letters to write. Let me know if you received those pictures.

                                    Your loving Son,
                                            A. E. Ehrke
                         League Island Navy Yard
                                  Philadelphia, Pa.
                             Aviation Barracks 263

THE "FLU" IS INCREASING

No one knows the cause of this disease.
It killed twice as many people in the United States last year as our armies lost in France.

IF YOU WANT TO PLAY SAFE:

1. Keep away from sick people, especially if they cough or sneeze.
2. Use your handkerchief when you cough or sneeze.
3. Avoid crowded street cars, trains, or houses.
4. Don't spit on the floor.
5. Wash your hands before eating.
6. Keep your fingers out of your mouth.
7. Avoid common drinking cups.
8. Keep out of dusty places.
9. SEE THE PLANT DOCTOR IF YOU ARE NOT FEELING RIGHT

International Harvester's 1918
influenza warning for their Milwaukee plant.
(Courtesy of the West Allis Historical Society)

The Spanish Influenza / Philadelphia's Naval Aircraft Factory

Nov. 14, 1918

Dear Folks:

Received your letter this morning and was sure glad to hear from you. You say Fred is home, is that right? Well tell him I sympathize with him. He sure has got hard luck.

We had a little accident up here yesterday—about 2,100 feet high and was coming down when one of the controls broke, and when we came about 100 feet from the water, we couldn't straighten out. So we went down in a nose dive. The pilot shut off the motors and let her go. We all wore life preservers—so as soon as she hit the water we got as best we could. All except one mechanic who never did get out. We were picked up by a tug about a half hour later.

The pilot had one arm broken, and I got a little cut on my leg. They brought a floating derrick over there and pulled out the machine-all broken up. The other mechanic was pinned in between the motor and the rest of the junk.

Crashed seaplane, but not Arthur's.
(Courtesy of the Naval History and Heritage Command)

You can't imagine how it feels coming down when you know there is no way to stop it. I thought of all kinds of things those few minutes it was coming down, but thank God it's all over and I'm still alive.

The Chief gave me a week off to rest up a bit, and believe me I sure need it.

Now don't worry about me, mother. I'm all right. I wasn't going to tell you about it, but I just had to.

Well, I'll close now, as I want to hit the hay.

Your loving son,

A. Ehrke

November 22, 1918

Dear Folks:

Just a few lines tonight to let you know that I'm still alive and everything is coming along fine. I went back to work today and everything was lovely. It makes my chest puff up a little to talk about that little flight we had—but it's to bad that Charlotte got killed—but that's all in the game and you got to take it as it comes.

This fellow was from Indiana and his body was shipped home the day they pulled him out. I remember when I was home I used to crave for excitement. I'm sure getting all I want now I guess.

I see Fred is on the job again at Akron and I suppose he's glad to go because he wrote to me and told me that Louie is gone and everything is dead up there. If I ain't mustered out by Christmas, I might come home on furlough.

How is the weather up there? It's pretty cold up here and when you're up about 3,000 feet, it's about 5 below zero.

Seaplanes in formation.
(NH 74090—Courtesy of the Naval History and Heritage Command)

The 27th of this month will be just six months that I've been in the Service, and if it takes another two months before I'm through, it will be eight months of my life in finding out something I didn't know-and something I always wanted to know-and that is how to hold your own among men and the value of money. That 's something I never knew before.

How's the bus-all set again I suppose? I sure would like to get behind the wheel again, and it won't be long and I'll be back-so take good care of it.

Lovingly your Son,
Arthur Ehrke
1511 Ritner St.
Philadelphia, Pa.

P.S. Tell him I'll write him tomorrow.

Letters Home from a WWI Seaplane Test Mechanic

November 29, 1918

Dear Folks:

Received the box Thanksgiving morning as I got out of bed and I sure done full justice to it. Two of my shipmates who were staying with me dug into it and it didn't last very long, but it sure was good-especially the coffee cake.

This place I'm staying at is with a private family and there are three of us staying in one big room. We are each paying $2.00 a week and eat outside. That's fair enough ain't it?

I'm sending a helmet, goggles, and a pair of gloves, which I want you to keep for me. It's the ones I wore on that little spill we had, and I thought it would be a pretty good idea to keep as a souvenir, and Dad can make good use of them on the car. Maybe he will have better luck than I had.

I'm sending a copy of the official transfer to the hanger. I've been working there about one month before we were officially transferred, and we went on subsistence from that day on.

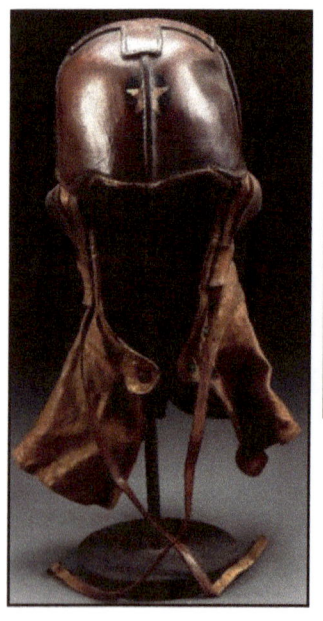

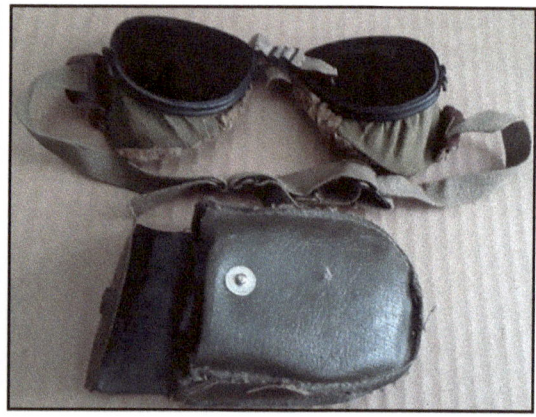

WWI aviation helmet and googles with case.
(Courtesy of ebay)

I'm feeling O.K. now, and am on another boat now, and believe me, I'm going to see that everything is right before I fly it. You can take that from me.

It's getting late, and I'll have to close. Tell Walter that I give the helmet and goggles to him.

Your Son,
A. Ehrke
1511 Ritner St.
Philadelphia, Pa.

Dec. 5, 1918

Dear Folks:

Received your letter today and was glad to hear from you. So Walter liked the outfit did he? I thought he would. I'm still out on the planes and flying everyday. We got new style helmets so I don't need that one. We haven't had any snow yet, but it sure is cold and we have some awful storms up here. Two of the planes we had anchored in the water turned over, and the force of the water tore them all up. These were of the pusher type with the propeller in the back and each one is worth about $32,000 dollars.

These big ones, like the one I'm on, cost about twice that much, but they can't turn over because they got too big of a wingspread. We had another little accident up here. One if the men got caught in a propeller and it cut him in just two pieces. They never did find him because he sank and the tide was going out at that time—so he is probably in the ocean someplace. Oh, it's a great life. When you see things like this with your own eyes, you forget about wishing for excitement.

All the machinist mates in aviation are not going to be mustered out, so I won't be home for some time yet. This river don't freeze up because there's too strong a tide, and they expect to fly all winter.

They are going to make a test trip with one of these planes to see just how long they can remain in the air. They want to stay up ten hours. There are going to be ten of us on the crew and we will take our diner with us. We will take up 650 gallons of gasoline, 70 gals. Of oil, and 100 gallons of water. If we stay up for ten hours, it will be the longest that any plane ever did stay up.

Believe me, this is just the kind of sport I'm looking for and something everybody can't do either. We got 30 Curtiss 8 cyl. motors to overhaul and 15 Liberty motors, including the two of the plane we fell in, so you see we got lots of work.

I've got lots of things I would like to tell you-but I can't even begin to write them. So, you will have to

N-1 Seaplane with Liberty 12-engine, Philadelphia Naval Aircraft Factory, 1918.
(NH 44116—Courtesy of the Navy History and Heritage Command)

wait until I get home. I'm feeling better than ever now, and this outside work sure agrees with me. Will close now, as I want to write Fred, so hoping you all feel as well as I do, I remain,

> Your loving Son
> A. Ehrke
> U.S.N.

> December 18, 1918

Dear Folks,

Received your box and am thanking you for same. Enjoyed it very much and whoever picked out those cigars sure got good ones-they don't handle the same cigars here like we got in Milwaukee, and a fellow don't know which ones to buy. If you ever send me another box, please don't send any candy. I don't care for candy anymore.

I was figuring on coming home on a furlough, but changed my mind. It would cost me $25.00 fare over and return besides the money I would spend when I got there. And I'll be mustered out in a few months, so I thought I might as well wait.

We are flying every day and it sure is cold. The first thing we do every morning is fill up with oil and gas, look over every wire, see that's there's a cotter key in every nut and safety wire on every turnbuckle, try the controls to see that they don't bind, see that there's no holes in the wings, test out the motors and put in water. That all takes about two and a half hours and then the pilot comes-and up we go for about one or two hours. Then come down, eat dinner, go back on the bus and make a few changes on something-maybe put in a different kind of oil or a new kind of a propeller, or if we are trying out the wireless-make a few changes on there, or maybe hook up the controls differently. All little changes like that. You see, we are the only Experimental Station and they try all kinds of things, and the only way to test these things is to take them up and if they don't work-you're out of luck, that's all.

That's how we happened to fall that time we made a change on the Aileron control. Then are flippers, one on each end of a wing, and they usually had one wire to pull it up and another to pull it down, and they figured that the weight of the flipper would bring it down without pulling it, so we took off the wire and it worked good on the water, but when we got up, it jammed, and they found out it didn't work, so we came down-all in one bunch. That is the beauty of a plane-no matter what happens you will always come down.

We made that ten-hour test I was telling you about and didn't have any trouble at all, but it sure was some grind. I was just about frozen and couldn't hear anything for about five hours afterward. We were up from 7 o'clock in the morning until 5 at night-and you got to keep your ears and eyes open and always hear the roar of the engines. It's enough to drive you crazy. We used all but 15 gallons of gas-so you see how close that was figured. We covered about as much space as from here to home—about 1,200 miles, but we stayed in a twenty-mile course. The air must be worn out over there. We are trying out a Duesenberg motor in these planes. Each motor has 16 cylinders and each cylinder has 4 valves. I don't know how they will work, but they look better than the Liberty motor.

I've got a lot of things to tell you, but it takes too long to write it, so I'll have to quit.

Your son,

A. Ehrke

Note: The longest leg of the first trans-Atlantic flight, which the US Navy accomplished six months later, was 1,200 miles. Arthur and his crew had just tested their seaplane's ability to travel that far before the Navy would try to cross the Atlantic Ocean. A map of the trans-Atlantic flight plan and the miles traveled between stops is located on page 92.

Duesenberg H Direct, V-16 Engine.
(Smithsonian National Air and Space Museum photo)

December 28, 1918

Dear Folks,

Just had my bath and it's only 3 o'clock, so I'll have to answer some of my neglected mail. I had a very nice Christmas here, but would have had a better one at home. I paid $2.50 for my dinner, but it didn't begin to fill me up. I eat more now than I ever did. I don't know what it is, but it just seems that I can't get enough. I think it's the outside work that does that.

I was supposed to fly one of the boats to Hampton Roads, Virginia last Tuesday, but we had engine trouble and couldn't go. I'm Chief Mechanic on this boat, so I had to fix it. The trouble was in the carburetors, and to fix it, I had to take them off—and remember, it was 5 degrees below zero—a stiff wind blowing and snowing like the devil. It took me all day Wednesday to take them

U.S. Naval Air Station, Hampton Roads, VA.
(Courtesy of the Hampton Roads Naval Museum)

off, and I swore about every curse I knew before they did come off and almost froze to death. Well Thursday I cleaned them and put in new jets. Friday I put them on, and it was harder to put them on than take them off. Well I got them on about 4 o'clock—that's quitt'n time. I spent Saturday morning in testing out the motors and they turned up 2,000 R.P.M. and I reported them O.K. and the Inspector will look them over Monday morning and I suppose we will make the trip then.

Hampton Roads is only 300 miles from here but it will make a nice little trip. It will take about three hours to make the trip barring trouble. The emergency rations we take along consist of six slabs of sweet chocolate and five gallons of drinking water. We only use that in case we get stalled some place and can't get nothing to eat and drink.

I'll stay at the Roads over Monday and Tuesday and will write just as soon as we land providing we leave Monday. I've got this motor game down to a science now, and I think after I get home I'll follow it up in connection with the machinist trade, and if Fred knows all he says he does with his blacksmith trade, we ought to be able to run a business of our own and that's what I'm going to do, as soon as I rake up the necessary funds. What do you make of it?

Well don't be surprised if you see me come home in a Chief's uniform because that's what I'm coming home in. I've moved since I wrote last-they didn't have enough light in the other place. I'm living at 1519 Green Street now and like it much better.

Say Walter, are you listening? I like your paper very much and you must write real much now. I didn't send you a present did I? Well, I'm coming home soon and will bring you a lot of them then.

Well, I'll close now, wishing you all a prosperous New Year.

Your Son,
Arthur Ehrke
1519 Green St.
Philadelphia, Pa.

Jan. 1, 1919

Dear Folks,

Just returned from Hampton Roads, Va. To find a big box on my dresser addressed from home. It sure made me feel good. After a fellow eats in restaurants for a while, then eats some homemade cake, cookies and bread, you sure find a difference.

I dug right into it as though I hadn't eaten for a month and believe me I did full justice to it.

I had a very nice trip, but it was pretty cold. I had to chew tobacco to keep my jaws moving. We left at 9 o'clock Monday morning and were scheduled to arrive there about 12, but we had engine trouble and were delayed 2 hours. Gas lines were clogged. We got fixed and were off again, arrived there at 2:30. I stayed there until Tuesday noon and took the 1 o'clock train for

U.S. Naval Air Station, Hampton Roads, VA.
(Courtesy of the Hampton Roads Naval Museum)

Philly arriving here at 11 o'clock just in time for the big night.

I expect to go there again Thursday on another boat. We are flying most of our boats to Hampton Roads because they have a stronger tide there and less apt to freeze.

Everything is lovely up here. Feeling better than ever. I expect Fred is having a good time in West Allis with the rest of the boys, but I'll be home soon, and have some of it myself.

I suppose you have the car stored away for the winter. Well don't forget to heat up your motor after you drain your radiator and keep your battery in a dry place. And it wouldn't be a bad idea to grease up certain parts so they don't rust.

Must close now, hoping to see you all soon,

Your loving Son
Arthur
1519 Green St.
Phila. Pa.

Art (in the bow) with his crew (family photo).

Art shown with goggles. Art's crew (names unknown).

Letters Home from a WWI Seaplane Test Mechanic

Jan. 10, 1919

Dear Folks:

I am enclosing a few pictures of some of our boats and also the one I fell in with. See if you can find me on them.

Everything is coming along lovely and working every day. It's 18 degrees below zero here, and it's rather uncomfortable flying in this weather.

I haven't much time just now as I just crawled out of the feathers and must go to work, so excuse the briefness.

Your loving Son,

Arthur

January 31, 1919

Dear Mother:

Received Della's letter and was very sorry to hear that you had the Flu. Also, she writes that you haven't heard from me in two weeks. Now I can't understand that at all. I sent a letter a week ago with some pictures in it, and I also sent a letter a few days ago stating that I was coming home on furlough the 10th of February.

Now I don't know why you didn't get them. Now if you are very sick, why I can home at once-if not, why I'll leave here the 10th.

We are having ideal weather up here and I'm feeling better than ever. There ain't much doing around here now, only overhauling motors and keeping the stove warm.

We got a big cooper kettle down at the hanger and have hot coffee all day long.

One of the ships came down the Delaware with 2,100 men from France. I haven't got any more news to write about

Arthur Ehrke, proud in his uniform.

During WWI, the German boat *Prinz Eitel Freidrich* failed to leave port as prescribed by international law in 1915. Interned at the Philadelphia Naval Yard, it was later reconditioned and refitted as a transport ship when United States entered the war. On May 12th, 1917, it was commissioned and renamed the *USS DeKalb*. The ship Art saw may have looked this one.
(NH 54659—Courtesy of the Naval History and Heritage Command)

but will have a lot of things to talk about when I get home.

So, I'll close, wishing you speedy recovery, I remain,

                                        Your loving son,

                                        Arthur

                    Fred J. Eisemann
                    NAVAL AIR STATION
                    Akron, Ohio

                                        Feb. 16, 1919

Dear Friend Della:

I suppose you will be surprised to get a letter from me without an invitation to write, but please don't think I'm trying to start a correspondence by writing this. Of course, I don't mean to say that I would not care to correspond with you. Indeed, nothing would please me more, but you understand I'm not pressing you unless you would really care to correspond. Which more likely, you would not, with me being a well, rube and everything.

But my purpose in writing this was to find out if Art is at home or still in Phila. I have something of importance to both of us to tell him. I had a letter from him saying he might stop off here on his way home the tenth of this month. He never came tho, and I don't know if he is at home or where he is.

Now, if you will write and tell me, I can write to him. You see I want to write as soon as I can. That is why I wrote you instead of trying first one place and then the other.

I heard your mother had the flu, and I hope that she has recovered by now. If you feel in a way offended at my writing to you, please pardon me, because I didn't mean to be rude.

If Art is home, will you please tell him I can not get my release for at least a few months at best. I want to thank you for your trouble because I feel sure you will do this for me, and write to me as I have explained myself as best I could.

Pardon the look of this note, as I must get out on the hop.

Sincerely,

Fred Eisemann

Fred Eisemann and Arthur Ehrke.

Letters Home from a WWI Seaplane Test Mechanic

While Art was at home, Fred wrote the following letter to him.

NAVAL AIR STATION
Akron, Ohio

February 22, 1919

Dearest???

Well kid-how are you getting on? Are you stepping out amongst them in West Allis any? Hope you don't get crowded or anything with social duties and the likes o'that. Anyway don't let them -.you.

And listen here darling, when in hell are you coming to see me? If you can't make it, why I'll get a furlough and cruise to Philly awhile.

I can get pretty near anything in a week or so. One of my henchmen will be my officer in a little while and I'll be sitting pretty. Now if you can stop off awhile here, we'll go to Cleveland. It's not forty miles away from here.

Listen if you are still there, call Kilbourn 2072R and ask for Frank. Tear out with him awhile and I think you'll have a good time. He's got a lot of jack you hold.

Well, maybe you'll be gone by the time this reaches there and it will be all H. S. (horse shit)

And kid, will you please tell your sister not to be sore or anything for me writing her. Always take a Dutchman as he means is the old saying. Now I would sure as hell like to have her write to me better than anything I know of, but that is for her to decide.

Your darling,
Fred

```
TELEPHONES {501
             502  MADISON SQUARE
             503}
CAFE 6628
```

Hotel Belmore
61-63-65 LEXINGTON AVE.
COR. 25TH STREET
New York

February 27, 1919

Dear Folks:

No doubt you are wondering why I don't write-- well the fact is I'm too busy. I arrived here Monday morning at 4:30-- all in. I slept all day and went to work Tuesday and we had to go to New York to assemble a plane to show at an exhibition. We had three motor trucks all packed and left Tuesday at 9 o'clock for New York.

We drove all that day and night-- never had an eye closed and we arrived here Wednesday noon and began unpacking and assembling. This is Thursday night and I haven't had any sleep for 48 hours-- so you can just imagine how I feel.

We might stay here one week or we might stay here six weeks-- don't know.

I'm staying at the BELMORE Hotel and it costs me $1.50 a night for one room. I'll have to close now as I can't keep my eyes open anymore. If you answer this letter, write to this address.

                HOTEL BELMORE
                61-63-65 Lexington Ave.
                Corner 25th St.
                New York

                                          Your Son,

                                          Art

New York City-SW corner of 3rd Ave. and 25th St., 1918.
(New York Public Library catalog ID (B-number): b16177190)

Hotel Belmore circa 1936.

Arthur kept extensive seaplane operation and maintenance notes, which start here and will continue in the following chapters. His notes and graphic designs are written with care and good penmanship, as was custom a century ago. Art also started a diary, and you will be able to view his writing yourself toward the end of Chapter Four.

```
                    United States Naval Air Station
                          Bay Shore, Long Island
Telephone Bayshore 324    List of tools and equipment for
                     operation and maintenance of seaplanes.

One Gasoline funnel with chamois skin strainer,
One Oil funnel with fine wire mesh strainer,
One Water funnel,
One Water filling can (5 Gallon Can),
One 1 Gallon Oil Measure,
Two 5 Gallon Gasoline Cans,
One 1 Pint Oil Squirt Can,
One 1 Pint Squirt Can for priming V2 Motors,
Three Pairs feelers or thickness gauges,  Three Pairs Wading boots/
One pair gas plyers,
One Pair Side cutting plyers,
One Pair end wire cutters,
One 3 inch screw driver,
One 10 inch screw driver,
One hack saw frame,
Six hack saw blades,
One Magneto Screw Driver (Dixie)
One Magneto Wrench (Dixie)
One set of propeller removing wrenches,
One blow torch,
One spool #20 copper wire for safety wireing,
One spool #30 copper wire for wrapping terminals,
One 1/2 lb. ball pien hammer,
One 1 lb. ball pien hammer,
Four open end wrenches sizes 1/4-5/16-3/8-7/16-1/2-9/16-5/8-11/16.
One 2 1/2 lb. Copper Hammer,
One Small Flat Chisel,
One Small cape chisel,
One small drift,
One center punch,
One breast drill,
One set drills from #1 to #60,
One Pair tin snips,
One cotter pin puller,
One Spark Plug wrench double ended,
One #5 sterling wrench,
One #2 Sterling wrench,
One 1/2 pound soldering iron,
One 1 pound soldering iron,
One pint muriatic acid,
Two small vaseline brushes,
Two small files - round and flat,
One pontoon hand hole plate wrench,
One 8 foot elbow or extension rule,
One pair goggles,  One life jacket,  One leather helmet,
One 5/16" socket wrench,  One 3/8" socket wrench,
One Zenith Carburetor Jet wrench.
```

NC-4 drydocked at the Naval Aircraft Factory.
(NH 2882—Courtesy of the Navy History and Heritage Command)

NC-4 seaplane and crew at the Rockaway Naval Air Station, New York preparing to cross the Atlantic in spring 1919. The wingspan of this seaplane was larger than a Boeing 727 of today. Fully loaded, it weighed 24,000 pounds and was powered by three Liberty tractor engines that generated 1,200 HP.
(NH 112451—Courtesy of the Naval History and Heritage Command)

Chapter Four
The Spanish Influenza Wanes and US Seaplane First to Cross the Atlantic

Unfortunately, a hundred years ago, the best microscopes could not see a virus. As a result, the medical community never knew what a virus was or how to combat it. For a pandemic to end, J. Alexander Navarro, a medical historian said the disease must fail to find enough hosts to catch it to spread it. Experts estimate that 500 million people around the world, or approximately one third of the world's population, contracted the Spanish Influenza. Fifty million people worldwide and 675,000 Americans died of the Spanish Influenza.

The Armed Forces Institute of Pathology chart shown on the opposite page indicates which cities were hit the hardest. As fate would have it, Art arrived in Philadelphia just before the Liberty Loan Parade, which attracted over 200,000 people. This parade became America's first "super-spreader" event in late September of 1918. Twelve thousand people died in Philadelphia in October 1918 alone. By March of 1919, when Art's letters continue, he was the lead mechanic on the Naval Factory's Seaplane float in future Liberty Loan Parades.

The first two waves of the Spanish Influenza occurred in the spring and then the summer and fall of 1918. During the war, the US Navy lost 431 men in combat but 4,158 to the Spanish Influenza.[1] The third wave

---

[1] "Influenza of 1918 (Spanish Flu) and the US Navy," NHHC archival document

Chart comparing mortality in Philadelphia with other cities.
(Reeve 3141, courtesy of the National Museum of Health and Medicine, Armed Forces Institute of Pathology, Washington, D.C.)

of the pandemic lasted six months and ended in June of 1919, resulting in the death of tens of thousands of Americans. In the spring of 1920, a fourth wave hit Detroit, Milwaukee, Kansas City, Minneapolis, and St. Louis hard, with significant death rates. However, by 1921, the death rates around the world returned to pre-pandemic levels.

A study co-authored by Markel and Navarro, published in the *Journal of the American Medical Association* in 2007 said that the US cities that implemented one or more of the recommended public health measures during the Spanish Influenza epidemic earlier and kept them longer in place had better, less deadly outcomes than cities that implemented fewer control measures. Eerily similar to Covid strategies, the methods used a hundred years ago included: masks, frequent hand washing, quarantining, and isolating patients. Closure of schools, public spaces and non-essential businesses were also employed. However, once the Spanish Influenza died down, the forgetting began.[2]

There are many possible reasons why America forgot about the pandemic so quickly. Some experts say most of the victims in United States died within a nine-month period. Additionally, the general population was familiar with pandemic patterns from typhoid, yellow fever, diphtheria, and cholera from the late 19th and early 20th century. Since the media was primarily focused upon the war effort, Americans were used to significant causalities and prolonged suffering.

In addition, when the Armistice occurred in November 1918, everyone wanted to celebrate the end of the war and embrace peace. Unfortunately, this pattern of forgetfulness and returning to normalcy seems to be repeating as the Covid pandemic winds down. Just as the influenza of 1918 never really left us and morphed into future flu viruses, experts expect Covid will remain with us for some time to come.

Now let's return to Art's letters just before the NC-4 seaplane became the first airplane to cross the Atlantic. The following information about the first seaplane to cross the Atlantic Ocean was inspired by two articles and the book, *A History of US Naval Aviation* by Capt. W. H. Sitz USMC. Edward Magnani published his article for

---

[2] Crosby, Alfred, *America's Forgotten Pandemic: The Influenza of 1918*. Cambridge University Press, Cambridge, UK 1998.

History.net on 5-8-19, one hundred years after three seaplanes left Long Island, New York, which was entitled *"The U.S. Navy's Curtiss NC-4: First to Cross the Atlantic."* The other article was written by *Aviation History, A Project of the Coast Guard Aviation Association* to document the historic "1919-NC-4 Transatlantic Flight."

In 1913, Lord Northcliffe, the wealthy owner of the *London Daily Mail*, offered 10,000 pounds sterling ($50,000) to the first airplane to make the first successful trans-Atlantic flight. He cancelled the offer during WWI but re-offered it afterwards. The US Navy went all in on the race even though Lord Radcliff changed the rules after the war, eliminating any mid-ocean stoppages, which knocked out the NC-4 from the prize money. This did not deter the Navy from its desire to become the first to accomplish this feat.

During WWI, American seaplanes were used to combat German submarines and had to be shipped overseas. The first US planes were no challenge to the Germans and were quickly shot down. Then Rear Admiral (RADM) David Taylor, Chief of the Navy's Construction Corps, decided the United States needed a flying boat capable of carrying bombs, depth charges, and defensive armament, with a range to enable it to fly from US to Europe. Glenn Curtiss and his engineers immediately designed a three- and five-engine aircraft to do just that. The NC-1, NC-2, NC-3, and NC-4 had large tail assemblies supported by hollow wooden booms rooted in the wings and hulls high enough to weather the high seas during takeoff. NC was shorthand for Navy-Curtiss and the newsmen of the day nicknamed them the "Nancies."

The Curtiss Aeroplane and Motor Company later modified its "flying boats" to three Liberty engines with one pusher to add more power. Space was allowed for a mechanic to service each engine to accommodate any in-flight problems. Art was one of those in-flight mechanics who tested these planes at the Navy Factory in Philadelphia where they were built to get them war ready and eventually trans-Atlantic worthy. He talks about the trans-Atlantic flight in his letter on May 5th, 1919.

The Navy's first attempt to cross the Atlantic was scheduled for May 6th, the next day, but the press wasn't told ahead of time. Unfortunately, a series of unusual events immediately occurred before they started. First, the NC-2 was damaged during take-off for its pre-flight test. Then a fire broke out at the Rockaway Naval Air Station on May 4th and damaged the NC-1 and NC-4. Parts from the NC-2 were used to repair the two damaged planes in an around-the-clock effort to get at least three planes working. The NC-3 was chosen as the flagship.

Their first leg started at Cape Cod and then they flew to Halifax, Nova Scotia. The second leg took them to Trepassey Bay, near St. Johns, Newfoundland. The third leg covered 1,200 miles to Horta in the Azores, and the fourth leg was a short hop to Ponta Delgada also in the Azores. The fifth leg brought them to Lisbon, Portugal. After they crossed the Atlantic, the NC-4 then flew to Plymouth, England, to complete the sixth leg. The Navy went all in with meticulous planning and ship deployment—similar to what United States did when NASA astronauts landed at sea upon their return after walking on the moon in 1969.

In 1919, however, radar had not yet been invented so the Navy enlisted five battleships as weather stations and destroyers were placed at fifty-mile intervals along each ocean route. Each plane had a primitive radiophone with a twenty-five-mile range. A total of 50 ships formed a protective "picket line" across the Atlantic. Each destroyer had a radio direction finder, but unfortunately, they worked poorly. The destroyers made smoke during the day and swung search lights at night to help the pilots. Additionally, star shells were fired when the planes were sighted. The ships would contact the next destroyer in line with news of their sighting.

Due to the hanger fire at Rockaway Naval Air Station, New York, and needed repairs, the three seaplanes took off on May 8th, 1919. The NC-4 had only been in the air once previously and thus first leg was its "shakedown" flight. Of course, it didn't go well. After passing Cape Cod over open sea, the NC-4 had to shut down the center "pusher" engine because of an oil leak. The captain pushed on with his three working engines until another engine blew a rod.

Poor visibility made the sea landing hard and then to top it off, their radio failed. They had to taxi 80 miles to the Chatham, Massachusetts Air Station in choppy seas. Their two engines were replaced but Chatham only had one 400HP and one 300PH Liberty engine. They

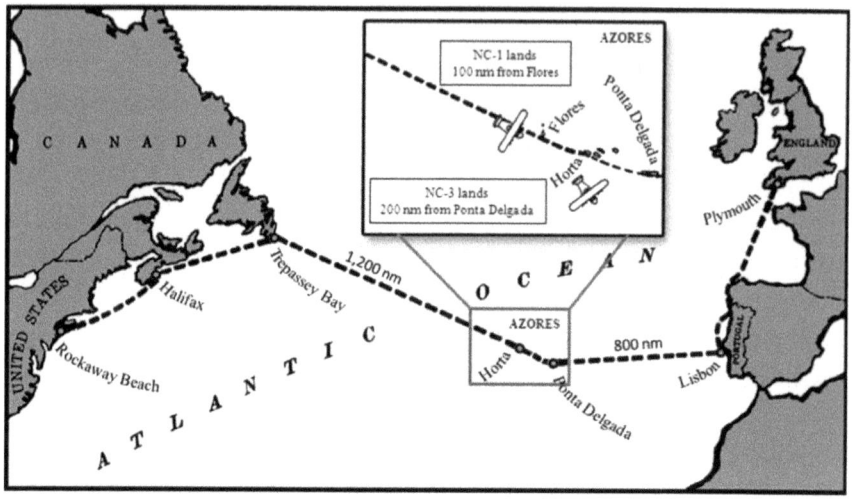

Map courtesy of the American Institute of Aeronautics and Astronautics.

forged ahead with what they had and planned to replace the 300HP Liberty with a more powerful one at Trepassey Bay.

Then, a 40-knot northeaster rolled in and delayed their departure from Chatham for six days. Due to their numerous problems, the newspapers dubbed the NC-4 the "Lame Duck."

Meanwhile, the NC-1 and NC-3 pressed on but also ran into heavy weather. Gusty winds buffeted them and damaged their new highly efficient Olmstead propellers. Luckily, they eventually reached Halifax. Once their cracked propellers were replaced with standard Navy ones, they left on May 10th. They followed the line of "station" ships and gazed at their first icebergs. Unfortunately, the air remained rough when the bitter cold set in. At Trepassey Bay, the swells were so high that their landing created an "avalanche of spray."

After the NC-4 left Chatham Air Base on May 14th, the center engine began to vibrate badly over open ocean, while the two outboards ran rough due to dirty carburetors. So, Lt. Stone, the NC-4 pilot, landed in Halifax rather than risk a night landing at Trepassey Bay. More bad weather ensued, so the NC-1 and NC-3 waited until May 15th to start the next leg. They planned to leave without the NC-4. However, as they attempted to take off for the next leg of their journey, the NC-1 and NC-3 could not lift off the water. The extra 200 pounds of fuel they took on for this long leg made them too heavy. The extra day it took to fix their mistake allowed the NC-4 to arrive and swap out engines to get their original 400HP replaced. Happily reunited, all three seaplanes took off for Horta in the Azores together.

The group followed the picket line of Navy ships throughout the night without incident until the weather changed. At dawn, low, thick clouds and dense fog made navigation suddenly extremely difficult. Then, as luck would have it, due to salt spray, the navigation lights on the NC-3 failed. As a safety precaution because it was impossible to get a reliable sextant of the sun, the three seaplanes spread out and moved out of tight formation to avoid a collision. Effectively blind and flying at one thousand feet altitude over open ocean, Flight Commander Tower, the pilot of the NC-3, saw a ship through a gap in the clouds and changed course, thinking he had lost then found his bearings.

Unfortunately, it was the wrong ship, which was a costly mistake. The pilot mistakenly followed the cruiser, *USS Marblehead*, which was returning home from Europe. Almost immediately, rain squalls, 22-mile-an-hour wind gusts, and thick clouds became so dense the pilot could not see his wing tips. The turbulent air then shook the seaplane so badly that his primitive instruments failed to inform him of his proper altitude.

Afraid of hitting a mountain on one of the islands he thought he was approaching, the pilot decided to land on the sea to get a radio-compass bearing. Unfortunately, he misread the cross swells and hit the

Flying boats NC-I and NC-3 at Trepassy Bay, Newfoundland, May 1919.
(NH 95777—Courtesy of the Naval History and Heritage Command)

NC-4 taking off from Trepassey Bay to the Azores.
(Courtesy of the Library of Congress)

ocean hard. The NC-3's stabilizing struts and center engine immediately buckled, which disabled any future flight. His now-damaged radio received messages but could not send any. Fortunately, the tides were favorable, so the pilot drifted and occasionally used his two working engines to eventually arrive at Ponta Delgada.

Sometimes when it rains, it pours. Commander Bellinger, the pilot of NC-1, made the same ill-fated decision as the NC-3 by following the *USS Marblehead*. To make matters worse, he was traveling at an altitude of 75 feet. At that altitude, accurate navigation and effective radio communication, were almost impossible. Flying blind, Bellinger lost the horizon and was ordered to land in 12-foot swells to get an accurate radio-compass bearing, which could only be performed while floating and had a 25-mile radius. Not unexpectedly, the pilot buried the NC-1 in a very large wave, which broke his wing struts and tail beams. The hull was also damaged, and the wings immediately filled with water. They started to sink. The crew immediately slashed any fabric in their way and bailed furiously. Through grit and courage, they survived for three hours before they were picked up by the Greek steamer, *Ionia*. Once they were safely onboard, the NC-1 immediately sank.

The following statement by one of Curtiss builders offers a glimpse of how fragile these seaplanes were and the remarkable skill the two NC-4 pilots who eventually flew over the Atlantic possessed. Dr. (CDR) Hunsaker, who helped create the NC-4, knew LCM Read and Lt. Stone, and described their skillset in his memoirs:

The NC-3 arrived at Ponta Delgada on May 19th, 1919 and sank three days later. (NC A2294—Courtesy of the Curtiss Aeroplane and Motor Company)

> *"The big boats had dual controls and the two aviators sat side by side and worked together on the controls which required strong effort at times. Read was a relatively small man, and he chose Stone because of his size and strength. The two were a good team. Stone had experience with flying boats, which were notoriously difficult to keep from stalling in rough air or at reduced speed. Stone also had experience in bad visibility weather. Stone had been a test pilot and knew how the crude instruments of the day could give indications contrary to the reliable "seat of the pants" signals of acceleration. On the eighteen-hour flight of the NC-4 to the Azores, Reed's function as a navigator required him to stand in the forward cockpit. Stone was in fact the chief aviator with Lt Walter Hinton sitting beside him as a partner."*

Of course, the NC-4 also struggled in the same gale that caused the NC-1 and NC-3 to crash into the sea. As flying conditions continued to deteriorate, LCM Read motioned to Lt. Stone to take the ship up because he was uncomfortable with the slow speeds and low altitudes during gale conditions. At 3,200 feet, they were able to break free above the clouds. As they approached the location where LCM Read thought where the next destroyer was stationed, he gave Stone orders to make a visual check.

As they re-entered the clouds, the plane began to buffet back and forth. Then a strong gust of wind hit, which made their wing drop. The plane immediately began to spiral down into a dangerous spin. Apparently, no one realized it until someone caught a glimpse of the sun through a break in the clouds. Read shouted to Stone to bring it out of the spin, which was no easy task.

Experts at the time said bringing a large heavily loaded aircraft out of a spin (the term "death spiral" had not yet been invented) in clear weather was quite an accomplishment all by itself. But re-entering solid clouds with zero visibility and pulling the plane out of a spin with the rudimentary flight instruments then available was truly an amazing feat.

Once Stone got the plane under control, he immediately went above the clouds again. Read stayed in the clear air and flew towards the islands using dead reckoning. In mid-morning the NC-4 passed through another opening in the clouds. What Read initially thought was a riptide turned out to be land. Spiraling down to 200 feet in complete control this time, he saw the southern tip of Flores, one of the western Azores. Ponta Delgada now was only 250 miles away and a picket destroyer shot off its star flare.

Shortly afterwards, the weather began to deteriorate again, and now their fuel was low. Rather than return to the clouds and dead reckon Ponta Delgada, LCM Read turned south to Horta on the island of Fayai in the Azores, where the *USS Columbia* was standing by. When they landed, the NC-4 received a tremendous welcome. Rain squalls and dense fog grounded them for four days, however, before they made their way to Ponta Delgada.

The governor, mayor, and a multitude of people greeted them. As luck would have it, the pilots and crew from the NC-1 and NC-3 had already arrived by ship, so they also congratulated them. On May 27th, 1919, the NC-4 pilots and crew got up at dawn and set off for Lisbon, Portugal. The weather was good and when the NC-4 passed over each destroyer, it messaged the *USS Melville* in Ponta Delgada and the *USS*

Rochester in Lisbon. They in turn forwarded NC-4's progress to the Navy Department in Washington. When the NC-4 saw the flashing lights from of Lisbon's Coda da Roca lighthouse, they knew they made it. Their welcome was tumultuous.

Early morning of May 30th, 1919, the NC-4 departed for Plymouth, England. When one engine overheated, they landed on the Mondego River in middle of Portugal. By the time it took to repair the leaky radiator, the tide had rolled out, which added to their delay. Since it wasn't safe to arrive at Plymouth in the middle of the night, LCM Read flew to Ferrol in northern Spain and spent the night there.

The next morning, as the NC-4 approached Plymouth, a formation of Royal Air Force seaplanes escorted them to the harbor. A British warship fired a 21-gun salute as the NC-4 circled to land. The Lord Mayor of Plymouth received LCM Read, Lt. Stone, and the crew. He escorted them to London, where they were decorated by the King of England. President Wilson, who was attending the Peace Conference in Paris, sent for them, congratulated them for their outstanding achievement, and introduced them to everyone in attendance.

In June 1919, Captain John Alcock and Lt. Arthur Brown of the RAF flew non-stop from Newfoundland to Ireland in a Vickers-Vimy bomber the following month. With the help of a sextant, whiskey, and coffee, the trip took in 16 hours before they unceremoniously crashed in

The NC-4, commanded by LCM Read, was photographed in Lisbon Harbor alongside the sea tender *Shawmut*. Newspaper headline:
"The only one of the Nancies to reach Lisbon—ironically—the *Lame Duck*."
(NH 95798—Courtesy of the Navy History and Heritage Command)

an Irish bog. After delivering the first trans-Atlantic airmail, they claimed Alfred Harmsworth's prize of 10,000 pounds sterling for the first non-stop trans-Atlantic flight. After his crash in Ireland, Alcock wrote, *"We have had a terrible journey. The wonder is that we are here at all. We scarcely saw the sun or the moon or stars. For hours we saw none of them."* Coincidentally, both Alcock and Brown were military pilots and prisoners of war. Throughout his time in prison, Alcock dreamt about how he would cross the Atlantic in a RAF Vickers-Vimy bomber and did just that.

Navy Secretary Daniels congratulates (from left) NC-1's Commander Bellinger, NC-4's LCM Read and NC-3's flight commander Towers, while Assistant Secretary of the Navy Franklin D. Roosevelt looks on.
(NH 53140—Courtesy of the Navy History and Heritage Command)

The previous stories about the first two trans-Atlantic flights were included to provide information about how primitive these first planes were. I still scratch my head when I think about Art's letter of December 18th, when someone noticed there were two wires that controlled the up-and-down motion of the rear tail flaps, which made the plane go up and down. On land, gravity made the flaps rest in the downward position. So, someone on the team thought the down wire was useless and cut the tail flap's down wire. Unfortunately, he did not factor in the plane's wind speed, which negated any downward action. As a result, gravity alone could not force the tail flap go down in midair. Real trouble ensued and Art's plane crashed for that reason alone. He describes what happened in his own words.

By March 11th, 1919, Art had established himself as a chief mechanic and eventually had 25 sailors reporting to him. His letter mentions his trip to New York to promote the Navy's Liberty Bond Spring Drive to pay for the war effort. Art was occasionally deployed at the Long Beach Naval Shipyard, where many of the crews for NC-1, NC-2, NC-3, and NC-4 trained before their trans-Atlantic adventure two months later on May 8th, 1919. His first letter of this chapter talks about the Spring Liberty Bond Drive that the Navy used to encourage citizens to buy US Saving Bonds to help pay for the war debt. Art was assigned to the Navy's PR campaign, in addition to his chief mechanic duties.

World War I poster depicting Lady Liberty. (Image courtesy of Library of Congress Prints and Photograph Division, LC-USZC4-8046)

Letters Home from a WWI Seaplane Test Mechanic

March 11, 1919

Dear Folks,

Received your long-waited-for letter and was glad to hear from you. I had a very nice time in New York and the show was a big success. It sure cost me a lot of money in New York, and I'll have to lay low for a while.

I only stayed in New York one week and three days. I'm in Philadelphia now and going back to New York this Friday to get the plane, and it will take about one week before we get through with the job.

You ask me if I'm in the Main Building. Now I don't get what you mean. You say they have a seaplane in Milwaukee now. If I were there now, I could explain anything you wanted to know about it. I suppose it is the one they had at the Lakes when I was there.

Well, that's just a small one. I've seen those Dirigibles collecting mail from the Garden, but that's old stuff because we have air mail service from Philadelphia to New York and I see it every day.

We are getting ready for the Spring Drive now and we are going to do a lot of flying. I expect to go to California by air and that will cover about 3,000 miles—and of course come back by rail.

I'm feeling very good, and we are having ideal weather. Will close now so I can gather a little sleep.

P.S. If you see Bussie, tell him to write.

Lovingly,

Art

Dirigibles circa 1925, Washington DC.
(Courtesy of the Library of Congress)

Letters Home from a WWI Seaplane Test Mechanic

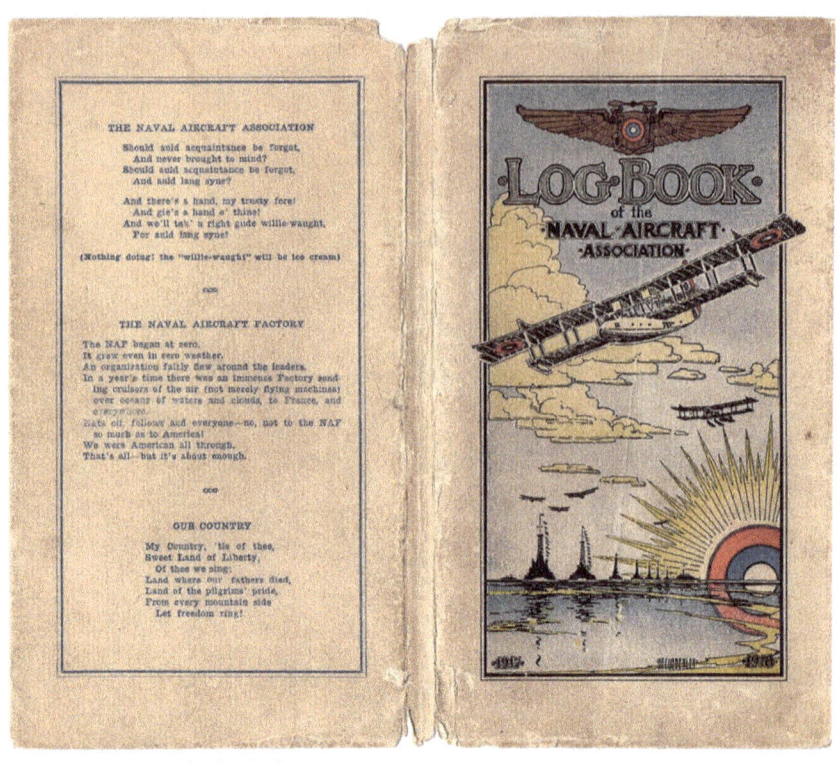

Logbook of the Naval Aircraft Association 1917-1918.

Arthur Ehrke is in the front row, fourth crew member from the left side.
On the top of page 68 of the logbook, (shown on next page), there is a tribute to Arthur.

> **LOGBOOK, N. A. A., 1917-1918** — 68
>
> We then have Ehrke, who was chief of the boat that carried the Liberty Bond riders, with Carlot and Smith for a crew.
>
> Now there comes a call for a boat—Shorty Souder is on the job and ready to man the oars, when our Chief West gives the command, in a hoarse, sea-going voice, "Shove Off." The crew is then brought ashore. Halpin has the tractor ready, the boat is put on its cradle by the boat men, pulled upon the ramp, where the crew goes over it, looking over every part before the next flight.
>
> "Chow" call now sounds, so we will have to eat, and we wish you all "happy days."

Logbook of the Naval Aircraft Association 1917-1918

                                                          March 21, 1919

Dear Folks,

Have not received any mail for two weeks. What's the trouble? We are commencing the Spring Drive now, and I'm flying most every day. I'm going to fly to all parts of the States this Summer and will have a lot to tell about when I come home again.

I suppose you're wondering why I don't send any money home. Well, the fact is that it cost me a lot of money to live the fifteen days in New York City, and as soon as I get straightened out, I'll send some. So don't think I'm forgetting.

We are having ideal weather down here and everything is going on lovely. I'm sending you the Logbook of the Naval Aircraft Association with a little write-up of each of the Crew. This was made before I got my higher rating.

I got a letter from Fred stating he was going to get a furlough and come to see me and we are going to Niagara Falls and New York City just to show him the burg.

> You might hear about me flying boats myself soon because
> I'm gradually coming to it. You know I'll soon be
> twenty-four years old*, and that's about old enough to
> handle one of these outfits.
>
> Hoping you're all enjoying the best of good health, I
> remain,
>
> Your loving Son,
>
> A.E. Ehrke

The Baptismal Certificate below indicates Arthur was born Sept. 17th, 1899, and shows he was nineteen years old when he wrote this letter. It's interesting Arthur mentioned he was twenty-four years to his parents, who knew better. I suspect due to wartime censors who monitored military mail, Arthur kept his lie about his age consistent to protect his career.

Spring 1919

Dear Father and Mother,

Just returned from work. I haven't had my clothes off or closed an eye since Thursday morning at 5:30 and it is 7 o'clock Friday night now. I worked all day Thursday, all night, and all day Friday. That's a nice little stretch, believe me.

I was flying all day Thursday and towards evening we got a message that four planes were coming from Cape May and we should watch out for them.

Well, one flew in about 8 o'clock at night and the pilot said that the other three were stalled all along the river. (Delaware) So we went out on the launch looking for them. We finally found one about two miles up the river and towed them in. When we had him anchored, we went out for the other one.

It was then 12 o'clock. We picked up the other fellow up about eight miles upstream and towed him in and then we started out for the last one with three search lights. We found him at 7 o'clock in the morning in a marsh—and the tide had gone down so he was high and dry and we couldn't get near him with the boat, so we cast anchor and laid there until 3 o'clock in the afternoon waiting for the tide to come in and float him.

Well, we finally succeeded in throwing him a heaving line and as soon as the tide came high enough, we were able to tow him. We landed in the hanger at 6 o'clock. Tonight, everything is O.K.

So you see this is no child's play—and believe me it sure was cold out on the river all night—wet feet and a stiff gale blowing, and no place to go to warm up. Oh, it's a gay life. I was engineer on this launch and we had a pretty bum motor, I so I didn't even....

(Unfortunately, the rest of the letter is missing.)

A 1918 Navy motor launch.
(Courtesy of the Navy History and Heritage Command)

Gustav Ehrke and friend looking over a car at the family home in West Allis, WI.
(family photo)

April 2, 1919

Dear Folks,

Received your letter and was glad to hear from you. So, the bus is all O.K.? Well, that is good. Now don't try to knock street cars off the track anymore. It don't pay—and it ain't much sport anyway.

I didn't send that Logbook as yet. It slipped my mind but I'll send it with this letter.

We were having some lovely weather up here the last few weeks, but I had a habit of leaving water in the radiators.

It turned awful cold one night and when I got to the hanger, I found the motor all frozen, and it took me all day to thaw it out. Nothing busted, but it was close to busting. I sure was lucky. I might of got summary court, but so far it's all O.K. and I ain't worrying.

I might be home on a furlough soon. Will let you know later. Will close now as my friends want me to go downtown, so excuse the briefness.

Your son,

A. Ehrke

May 5, 1919

Dear Folks,

Just a few lines to let you know everything is all right and I'm enjoying the best of good health. So, you have an Aviation Field [*established on July 3rd, 1919, pictured on the next page*] there now? That's nice. Well, that plane is just one-third the size of ours. So, you can imagine how large it is.

You say this fellow came down in a nosedive and broke a propeller. Well, I see you don't know what a nosedive is. If he came down in a nosedive—there wouldn't be anything left of the machine. When a plane is up in the air and comes straight down—nose first it's called a nosedive. All that fellow did was make a bum landing.

Milwaukee Historical Marker.
(www.WisconsinHallofFame.org)

There's rumors going around that we are going to be shipped to Honolulu. There's a new Naval Aviation Base there. I ain't sure, but that's what I hear. I ain't worrying over it either. I think I'd like it over there.

I might be home on a furlough sometime this June if everything goes right, and I'll bring Fred along. They're turning out one plane a day here—and it sure keeps us on the jump to keep them running, believe me.

Tomorrow is the day set for the Navy planes to leave for the Transatlantic flight—probably you heard something about them. The Navy entered four planes—the N.C.1, N.C.2, N.C.3 and N.C.4, and I believe the U.S.N. will be the first to cross. Anyway—I hope so. We don't want the English or French to beat us out.

Spanish Influenza Wanes / US Seaplane First to Cross the Atlantic

Lieutenant Commander Albert C. Read, USN (left), Lieutenant Commander Robert E. Byrd, USN, (center), and Lieutenant Walter Hinton, USN (right), with their NC-4 as they prepare for the trans-Atlantic flight later in Rockaway, May 1, 1919.
(NH 52839—Courtesy of the Naval History and Heritage Command)

CDR Towers taking command of the trans-Atlantic NC squadron on May 3rd, 1919.
(Courtesy of the Naval Sea Systems Command)

Just a minute (five minutes) till I load my pipe. All done, let's go. I'll send you those pictures in about one week. They aren't developed yet. I'm going out among them tonight, so I'll have to cut it short.

Your loving Son,
A. Ehrke

P.S. Mother, this is the best girl you ever met. Now don't think I'm going to marry her because I ain't that kind of guy.

May 10, 1919

Dear Sister,

Received your letter and am very glad you reminded me of Mother's birthday. I really didn't know when it was. I'll give you $10.00—that's all I can afford just now—so you buy her something for me.

I'm having some wonderful times and wish you were here to enjoy some of it.

Old dizzy Wimmer has been writing for some time—But I don't answer her letters. Can't be bothered.

I don't expect to get out of the Navy for some time and I ain't worrying over it either—flying every day and coming along fine.

Will have to close now as some of the boys want to go to town, so will cut this short.

Your loving brother,
A. Ehrke

Photo of his friend found in Art's belongings.

```
                                              May 13, 1919

Dear Folks:
                        ATTENTION

Now when I send you a picture of a girl—don't tell me
not to get married too young. Who was telling you I was
going to get married? You know better than to warn me of
such things. This guy ain't going to get married for a
long time yet, so forget about me getting married.

So having cold weather up there. Well, it's been cold up
here for the last few days—but it was awful warm up
here.

I've got twenty-five Sailors under me now and I have
charge of all the repair and testing of motors. So, you
see this ain't a small job. Everyday seems to be a holi-
day for me—and I think I was cut out for work like this.
```

I'm glad you've got your car tuned up because I'll be home in a few months to enjoy some of the West Allis air.

Fred says he's coming along all right and I expect he will come with me. I'll have to close now as I'm running out of news and time. So, nighty, nighty--

Your son,
A. Ehrke

May 1919

Dear Folks,

Received your letter, but sorry to say I was rather late in answering. Now I can't pull that "too busy" stuff anymore because I was just too careless, but I won't let it happen again.

Everything is lovely here and doing a lot of flying now that the weather permits. I got a little writeup in the paper, which will probably be of some interest to you.

So, you're making a garden—that sounds pretty good. Well, I can't help you make it, but I might help you eat some of its offsprings.

So, Schroeder got married, did he? Well, he don't know anything—and it's just as good for him to do that as anything else.

I'm expecting to fly to San Diego, California in a plane very soon, and I imagine it will be some trip.

Mr. Bernstein was rather surprised at me making Chief was he? Well, that's not saying much for me, but maybe he didn't mean it that way.

> I don't know when I'll get out of the Service, but I really ain't worrying over it. I could get out if I really want to push my request, but I'm going to stick here awhile. I'm getting some big ideas since I left home, and if it all works out right, I'll be O.K.
>
> I'll have to close, so will say good-night and don't take any wooden money.
>
> Your loving Son,
Arthur E.

Curtiss N-9 Seaplane.
(NH 74653—Courtesy of the Naval History and Heritage Command)

Art and pilot preparing to take off in an N-9.

Letters Home from a WWI Seaplane Test Mechanic

After the war, surplus training warplanes, called "Jennys" were sold for as little $200 and came in a box. A true bargain compared to their $5,000 wartime cost. Without government regulation, these planes became the backbone of postwar aviation in America, especially for barnstorming and rural mail delivery. Art was working on one for a friend and mentioned he was almost finished repairing it in his next letter on 6-16-1919.

June 16, 1919

Dear Mother:

Just received your letter and as I'm taking the day off, will have lots of time to answer it. You must have had a very nice parade down home according to your letter. We have some kind of parade most every day. It's getting to be old stuff.

I just got my new uniform last Saturday, and without the buttons and rating, it cost $45.00. The rating will cost about $5.00. it's a very nice piece of serge* and I think it will last me until I get out of the service.

We are building four N.C.1 planes down here and I got a very good chance to get on one to make a non-stop trip to Ireland. What could be better than that, eh?

We are getting along very nicely on that plane I wrote you about, and I expect to have it flying in another two or three weeks. We are now waiting for parts which are being shipped from Canada.

The Senators and Congressmen from Washington were down to the Navy Yard on a tour of inspection last week, and I had the pleasure of being on the boat which took them over to Hog Island to watch the Ship Launching.

So, Fred has been sending home for money? Well, he must be in hard luck. He told me about sending his wife to her aunt's—and I suppose she is costing him a lot of money. Well, the older he gets, the more he will earn, so let him go. I ain't discouraging him any, but he is beginning to realize what he has done, and I wouldn't be surprised if he wasn't working for a transfer to get away from Ohio.

An inside view of a plane similar to the one Art mentioned in his letter of June 16, 1919.
(Courtesy of the Smithsonian National Air and Space Museum)

He sent me a picture of his wife and another girl. She seems to be a very nice girl. I bet she just shook hands with him, and he got red in the face and married her.

But it's a gay world after all. Everything is going lovely, and I never felt better in my life. Hoping you all feel the same.

I remain Your Son
Arthur E.

Serge is a twill weave woolen fabric commonly used for military uniforms.

The NC-1 with the 51 men who set the world record for passengers in November 1918.
(NH 42552—Courtesy of the Naval History and Heritage Command)

Hog Island, Philadelphia Naval Yards.
(Courtesy of the National Museum of American History)

A little more than three weeks before his death, Arthur started a diary, which was returned to his parents with his belongings.

Philadelphia's Walnut Street Theater was founded in 1808 and is America's oldest theater.
A National Historic Landmark, this is a street view of the theater in 1913.
(Courtesy of Library of Congress, Prints & Photographs Division)

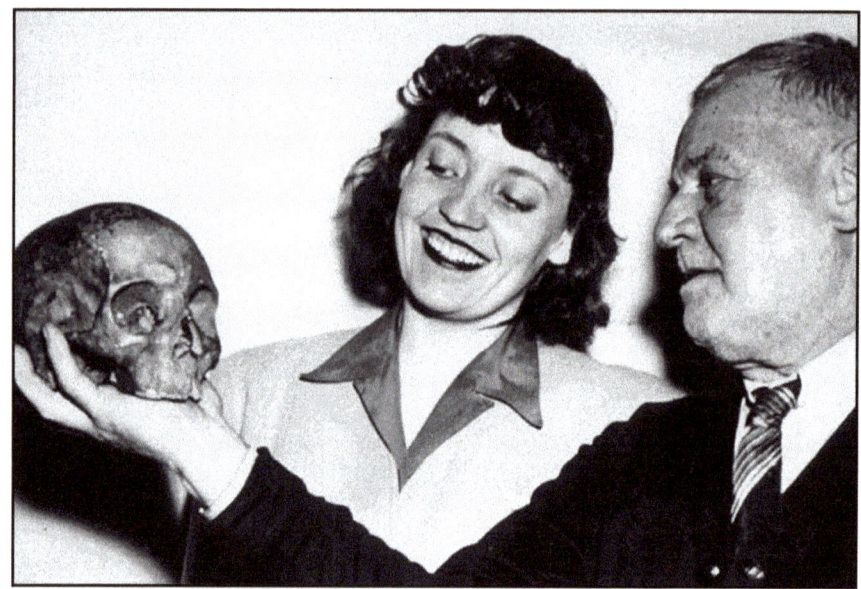

During a 1920 renovation when workman removed the old interior, they discovered an old relic from the early days of the Walnut Street Theater. One of them was the skull of John "Pop" Reed, a stagehand at the Walnut for more than 50 years in the first half of the 1800s. Reed stipulated in his will that he wanted his skull separated from his body, duly prepared, and used to represent the skull of Yorrick in *Hamlet*. His wish was granted, and the skull is signed by many famous actors of the day who performed in Shakespeare's play.
(Courtesy of the Walnut Street Theatre Archives)

Photochrom postcard of East Fairmount Park and the Schuylkill River circa 1923.
(Courtesy of the Beinecke Rare Book & Manuscript Library, Yale University)

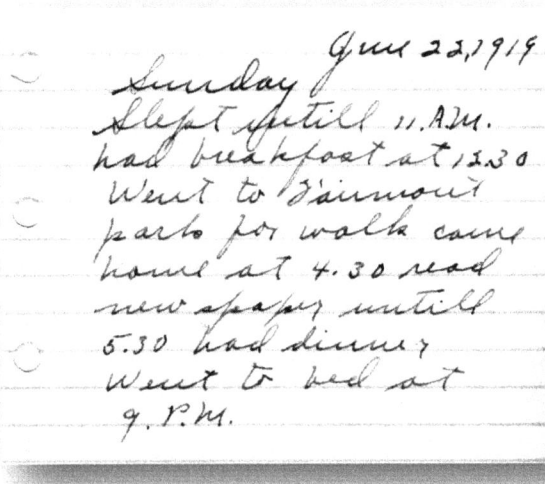

> Sunday June 22, 1919
> Slept until 11 A.M.
> had breakfast at 12.30
> Went to Fairmount
> park for walk came
> home at 4.30 read
> newspaper untill
> 5.30 had dinner
> Went to bed at
> 9. P.M.

AMAZING SIGHTS   THRILLING STUNTS
The NAVY YARD OPENS
TODAY, JUNE 28

Gates open at noon and close at 8 P. M.   Yard closed after this date.

See—Largest Aircraft Factory in the World, Trick Flying, Submarine Diving, Great New Dry Dock, Armored Cars used at Metz, Torpedo Boats, Chasers, Caterpillars, Launching Ways, Wireless Telephones, Submarine Listening Devices, Searchlights, Baseball Games, Tug of War, Boxing Contest, Greased Pig Race, Rowing Contest, Drill of the "Devil Dogs," etc., etc. etc.

First time the Navy Yard has been open to the Public since War was declared—see the great changes that have taken place.

DANCING, MUSIC, REFRESHMENTS.
(Dancing Stops at 9.30 P. M.)

Entire proceeds for the benefit of the Navy Relief Society, which cares for the widows and orphans of the deceased officers and enlisted men of the Navy and Marine Corps.

Street cars direct to the Yard every two minutes.
No cameras or packages permitted in the yard.

IT'S THE BIG SHOW
ONE FEE ADMITS TO EVERYTHING

Admission	$ .50
Children	.25
Automobiles and Parking	1.00

THIS SPACE CONTRIBUTED TOWARD THE SUCCESS OF
"NAVY RELIEF DAY" BY THE FOLLOWING:

Chas. Kranish & Co.	F. W. Whitaker & Co.	Jos. Lomax
C. M. Loeffler	Halcomb Steel Co.	Ellis Jackson & Co.
Bradlee & Co.	Fowles & Co.	Ketcham & McQuaide
Jacob Stern & Sons	Garrett-Buchanan Co.	Fred C. Koelle
H. E. Strathmann	Franklin Textile Mfg. Co.	J. H. Kerr
C. Sautter & Sons, Inc.	Child & Townsend	G. L. Littlewood & Co.
W. F. Hessel	Hub Machine W. & C. Co.	L. H. Manko
Van Dusen & Stokes Co.	J. H. Weil & Co.	Henderson & Co.
Belmont Packing & Rubber Co.	Keystone Screw Co.	New York Shipbuilding Co.
Uhler & English	Stanley Booking Co.	Betsy Ross Co.
L. D. Berger	Murphy & Co.	J. A. Roeblings, Sons Co.

Philadelphia Inquirer, June 28th, 1919.

Letters Home from a WWI Seaplane Test Mechanic

June 22, 1919

Dear Folks:

This happens to be Sunday, and as I ain't got anything to do—thought I would write a few lines. I've decided on not coming home this July. I won't be able to get a furlough, so I'll wait until August.

The 28th of this month is Navy Day in Philadelphia and the Navy Yard will be open to the Public. Admission will be 50 cents. They are going to have sham battles in the air, on the water, and below the water. We are going to do a lot of stunt flying also. I sure wish you were here to see it.

I've got a job promised we hear, working as a civilian for the Naval Aircraft Factory as Motor Mechanic when I'm mustered out. It's a civil service job and the pay is from 80 cents per hour up. I'm going to take it too. That's falling soft, isn't it?

Listen, Mother, I've got the beginning of a sore throat and I would like very much if you would send me a bottle of Hien Fong.* I can't get it here. It isn't sore yet, but it might be. ...

I might get an apartment with my roommate and try batching it for awhile. We can get anything we want to eat from the commissary store at the Navy Yard very cheap—and my friend is a very good cook.

It costs about $15.00 a week to eat in restaurants and you get sick of eating that stuff. Well, that's all I know just now, so I'll have to quit.

Yours as ever,

AE

Art did get his Hien Fong from home, but seven months later, various newspapers published the following three articles about Art's sore throat cure.

Hien Fong Essence or Green Drops is made in Rochester, Mich., by the Knorr Medical Co. The mouthwash has been produced in the Detroit area since 1881, said George Knorr, president and owner. The four-ounce bottle, which is 60 percent alcohol by volume, cost $1.

The Green Drops are especially popular in Milwaukee and among people of German origin, Knorr said. The liquid is bottled in the basement of a Rochester home, said a woman who answered the Knorr telephone.

Gilbertson of the FDA said alcohol is often used in these products to suspend the other ingredients.

Newspapers.com

Well, 55 Pct. Should Satisfy Most Anybody

(Chicago Tribune-New York Times Special to the Gazette.)

Chicago, Feb. 28.—Federal agents today laid violent hands upon two carloads of "Hein Fong Essence," a tonic with a Chinese name, a delirium tremens composition, and an army mule kick. The two carloads were consigned to wholesale druggists of Chicago. A chemical analysis showed that the tonic contains 55 per cent of alcohol. According to the federal authorities, the manufacture of the "tonic" is peculiar. "Hein Fong" is carefully filtered through layers of absorbent cotton until the herbs and other solids have been eliminated. The remaining mixture of alcohol, water and the essence of the herbs was ther ready for use and what it did to th tired business man, one or two shots of it, was said to be ample.

February 28, 1920, article
Newspapers.com

69 Per Cent Alcohol.

The Knorr Medical company, 612 Fourteenth avenue, was the other defendant named in the bulletin, the company paying a $50 fine after pleading guilty to misbranding "Knorr's Genuine Hien Fong Essence or Green Drops," consisting of 69.72 per cent alcohol, .35 per cent ether, non-volatile matter, and flavored with oil of spearmint.

The wrapper said the medicine "had proved its efficiency in diseases of the stomach and bowels, colic, cholera morbus, summer complaint, neuralgia, catarrh, grippe, colds, tonsilitis, sore throat, croup and diphtheria. For inflammation and weakness of the eyes it gives wonderful benefit, and dullness of ears, and even deafness has been relieved and benefited."

1916 article
Newspapers.com

Slogan of the Women's Christian Temperance Union. Produced in Thomas Edison's studio. © The Art Archive at Art Resource, NY

To provide background information, the Wartime Prohibition Act was passed on November 18th, 1918, which limited all alcoholic beverages to 1.28% alcohol to save grain for the war effort even though WWI had ended the prior week. The law took effect on June 30th, 1919, and thus July 1st became known as "Thirsty First." The US Prohibition Era began on January 17th, 1920, which may explain the Hein Fong bust on 2-28-1920.

> June 23, 1919
> Monday
> Put boat on ramp for alterations
> Was witness for general court martial of two pilots Ensign Burke & Lieut Thomas
> Flew Canadian boat for 25 minutes
> Quit work at 4 P.M.
> Read newspaper until 10 P.M. went to bed at 11 P.M.

Note: Arthur attended the court martial of two pilots, who attempted to fly a plane while intoxicated. Art led the testing crew assigned to them and the superintendent would not let the pilots fly that day. The next day, the pilots had their test flight, and everything went OK. Within three weeks, Art had to witness an additional two times at the court martial for these same pilots the day he died. The details of what happened and Art's concerns about them will be discussed in Chapter Five.

Curtiss MF-Boat—These seaplanes were used as trainers and support craft in WWI.
(Courtesy of the National Naval Aviation Museum)

Submarine Chaser #74.
(NH 42585—Courtesy of the Naval History and Heritage Command)
This is the boat that Art referenced in his June 24, 1919, diary entry.

June 24, 1919
Tuesday
Got up at 5.30 A.M.
had breakfast
pressed clothes
over hauled motor
on M.F. reset stagger
Submarine Chaser
#74 caught fire
right off of Hangar
Went out with launch
brought 40 men ashore
boat was salvaged
quits work at 4 P.M
had dinner wrote
letter to F.L.
went to bed at 9. P.M

A WWI wherry A wherry is a flat-bottomed boat that can easily be pulled onto a beach or river shore. It is propelled by either oars or sails to cross short distances like the Delaware River.
(Courtesy of the Norfolk Tales and Myths site)

> June 25, 1919
> Wednesday
> Pay day drew $30.00
> Got up at 6.30 A.M.
> launched # 3614
> painted wirries
> had lunch
> quit work at 4. P.M.
> had dinner took
> bath took Stella S.
> to theater had
> lunch took stella
> home at 1.30
> went to bed at 1.30 A.M
> got up at 3. A.M.
> caught 2 burglars on
> roof turned them
> over to police went
> back to bed at 4.30 A.M.

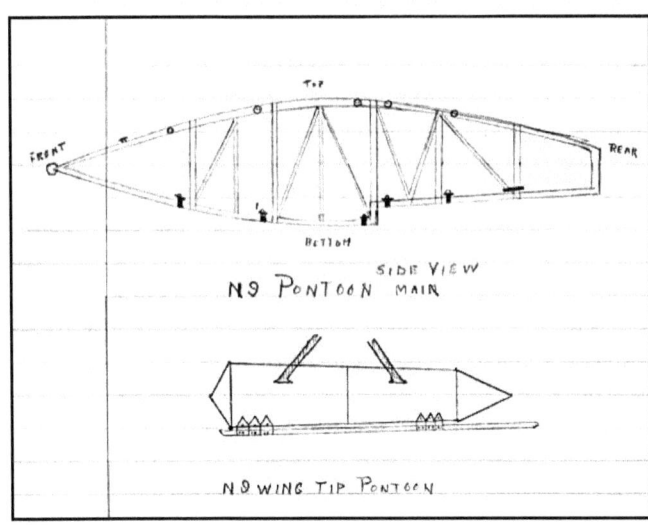

Art's sketch of an N-9 pontoon.

Letters Home from a WWI Seaplane Test Mechanic

> June 26, 1919
> Thursday
> Got up at 6.30 A.M.
> had breakfast
> got boat ready for
> flight started to rain
> did not fly sat
> around happy untill
> 4 P.M. had dinner
> read paper went
> to bed at 10.30 P.M.

The general public viewing the WWI battleships at the Philadelphia Navy Yard
on Navy Relief Day, June 28, 1919.
(NH 45292—Courtesy of the Naval History and Heritage Command)

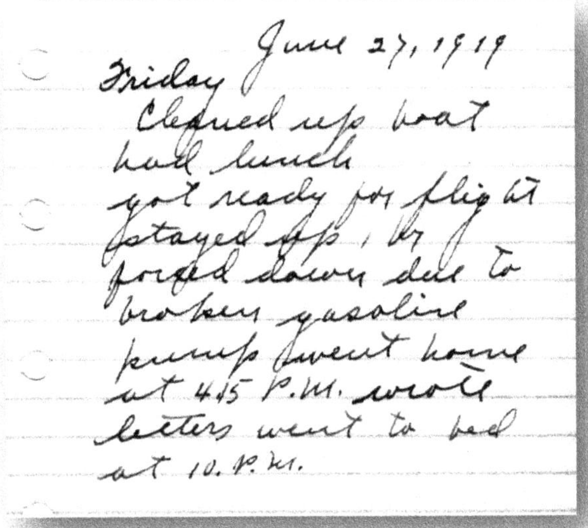

June 27, 1919
Friday
Cleaned up boat
had lunch
got ready for flight
stayed up 1 hr
forced down due to
broken gasoline
pump went home
at 4.45 P.M. wrote
letters went to bed
at 10. P.M.

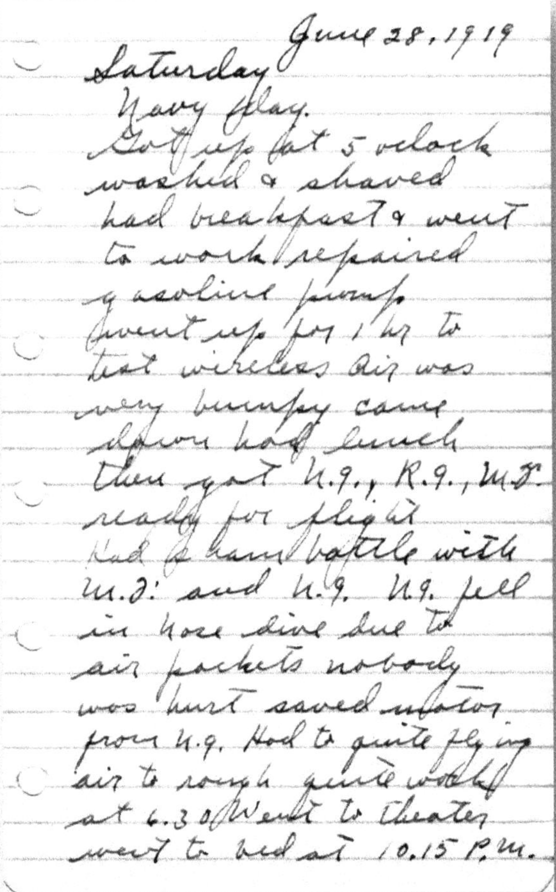

June 28, 1919
Saturday
Navy day.
Got up at 5 o'clock
washed & shaved
had breakfast & went
to work repaired
gasoline pump
went up for 1 hr to
test wireless air was
very bumpy came
down had lunch
then got N.9., R.9., M.F.
ready for flight
had sham battle with
M.F. and N.9. N.9. fell
in nose dive due to
air pockets nobody
was hurt saved motor
from N.9. Had to quit flying
air to rough quit work
at 6.30 Went to theater
went to bed at 10.15 P.M.

Letters Home from a WWI Seaplane Test Mechanic

Curtiss H-16 Seaplane about to be launched.
(NH 61148—Courtesy of the Naval History and Heritage Command)

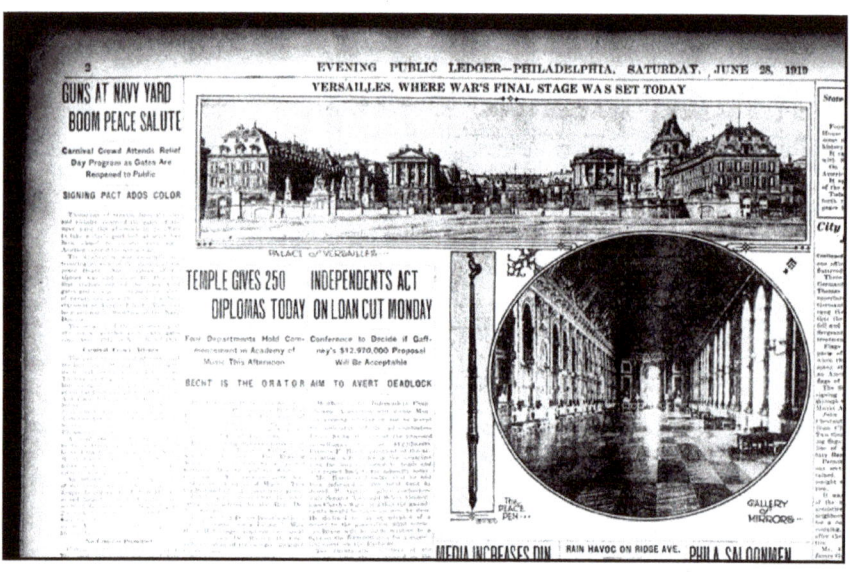

Philadelphia Evening Public Ledger, June 28, 1919.
(Transcription of the *Guns at Navy Yard* article follows.)

The transcription of the article:

GUNS AT NAVY YARD BOOM PEACE SALUTE

Carnival Crowd Attends Relief Day Program as gates are Reopened to the Public Signing Pact Adds Color

Thousands of persons from the city and vicinity swarmed the gates of the navy yard this afternoon in an effort to take a day's good look at what has been closed to curious eyes since America entered the world war.

The celebration was especially interesting in view of the signing of the peace treaty. Announcement of the signing was made about the time the first visitors reached the navy yard gates and was accompanied by a salute of twenty-one guns from the warships stationed at League Island. This had been ordered by Secretary of the Navy Daniels.

The occasion of the first opening of the marine guarded Navy Yard gates since 1917 is Navy Relief Day.

Carnival Crowd Attends

The gates were opened at noon, and the first comers thronged into the yards as several seaplanes soared overhead. Trolleys running at minute intervals bore its carnival crowds to the entrance of the yards, beginning before 11 o'clock. And those folks who left their homes before luncheon patronized thirty refreshment booths which are being conducted on the avenues of the Naval yard by yeomen and women prominent in Philadelphia Society.

A small admission fee was charged at the entrance, and the money will be used for the activities of the Naval Relief Society, which looks after the wives and families of sailors and marines who died in service.

An attraction which brought most of the curious to the back channel of League Island was the U-boat 117, the second largest of its kind in the surrendered German navy. Beginning at 2 o'clock, a submarine submerged every hour with the faithfulness of the geyser in Yellowstone to the delight of the spectators.

No Cameras Permitted

Certain restrictions were observed. The yard authorities announced that no one would be permitted to bring a camera to the yard. Nor were packages of any kind allowed, unless they were opened for inspection at the gate.

Otherwise, the thousands of visitors were free to wander at will through the yard, which has grown to be the largest naval station in the United States, and by far the most interesting because of the diversity and importance of the work done there.

Samuel Gompers, president of the American Federation of Labor, is expected to visit the yard in the afternoon.

Because the Navy Relief Society cannot afford to take a chance of losing money on Navy Day, its offices went to the trouble of insuring against rain with Lloyd's agency, the noted British insurance institution. To get data Lloyd's needed to underwrite Navy Day, the government established a meteorological observatory at the yard.

The Philadelphia Rapid Transit Company is co-operating with the Navy officials to make the day a success by putting on an extra car service. The P.R.T. has announced that service on routes to the navy yard has been increased 100 per cent for the occasion.

On Routes 2 and 20 the schedule has been arranged in such a way cars arrive at League Island at less than one-minute intervals. These were fifteen to twenty additional cars held in readiness all day to meet any sudden emergency.

To keep the cars to League Island moving, supervisors were stationed at various points along the routes. Every effort was made to handle all passengers, who wish to go to the navy yards, both speedily and comfortably.

Beats Circus

No three-ringed circus ever offered the diversified entertainment that was provided visitors this afternoon.

For the first time the public saw the great changes that have taken place. On view also were battleships, destroyers, submarines, submarine chasers, guns, caterpillars, tractors, aeroplanes…everything that was used in the war.

To make the day interesting a program included trick flying, submarine diving, wireless telephones, search lights, athletic games, boxing, baseball, dancing and a diversity of sports and amusements.

> June 29.1919
> Sunday
> Got up at 8.45 A.M.
> had breakfast
> read newspaper untill
> 12.30 P.M. had lunch
> slept for 2 hours
> read newspaper untill
> 5.30 P.M. had dinner
> went to Strawberry
> mansion then to
> Woodside park went
> to bed at 11 P.M.

1913 postcard of Strawberry Mansion within Fairmount Park, Philadelphia.

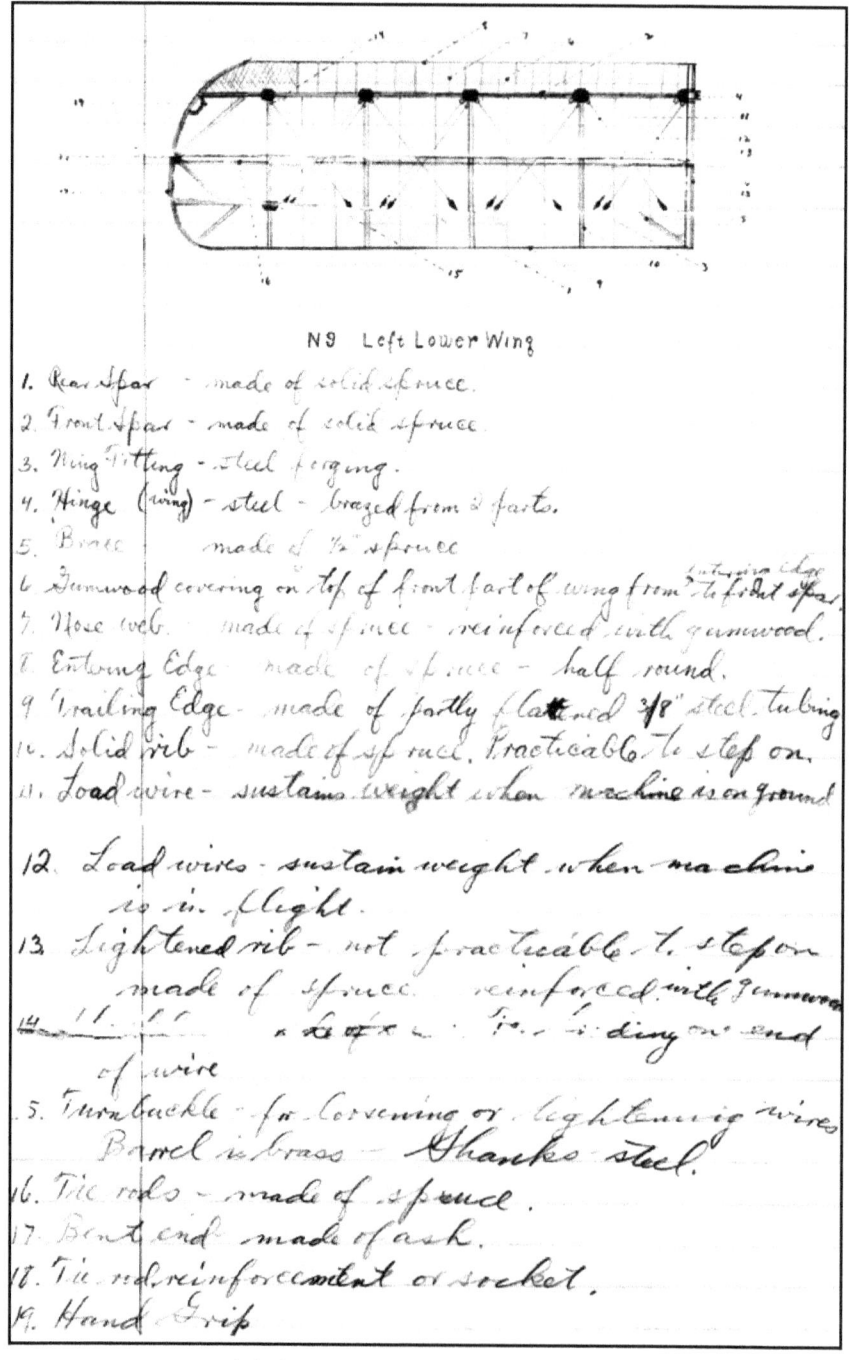

N9 Left Lower Wing

1. Rear Spar - made of solid spruce.
2. Front Spar - made of solid spruce.
3. Wing Fitting - steel forging.
4. Hinge (wing) - steel - brazed from 2 parts.
5. Brace - made of ½" spruce
6. Gumwood covering on top of front part of wing from entering edge to front spar.
7. Nose web - made of spruce - reinforced with gumwood.
8. Entering Edge - made of spruce - half round.
9. Trailing Edge - made of partly flattened 3/8" steel tubing
10. Solid rib - made of spruce. Practicable to step on.
11. Load wire - sustains weight when machine is on ground
12. Load wires - sustain weight when machine is in flight.
13. Lightened rib - not practicable to step on made of spruce reinforced with gumwood
14. "   "   " soft wood for winding on end of wire
15. Turnbuckle - for loosening or tightening wires Barrel is brass - Shanks steel.
16. Tie rods - made of spruce.
17. Bent end made of ash.
18. Tie rod reinforcement or socket.
19. Hand Grip

Arthur's notes about the Curtiss N-9 seaplane.

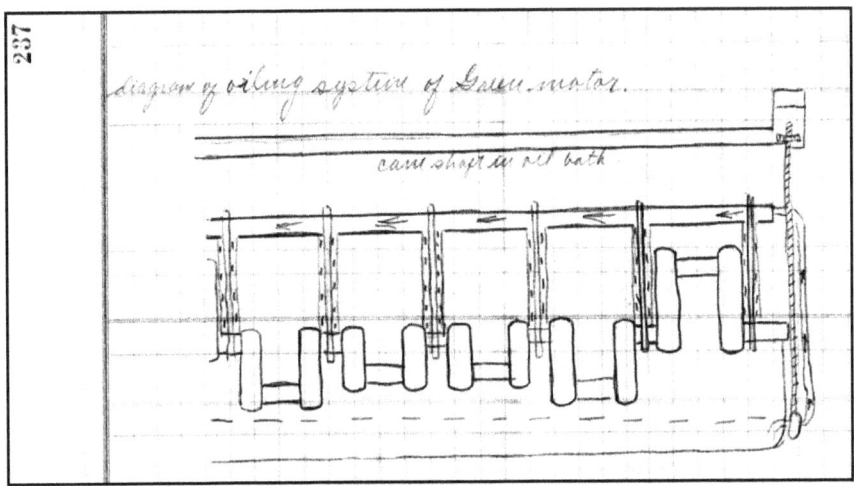

Arthur kept detailed notes of each engine's specifications and tolerances. This is a Green Motor cam shaft in its oil bath, but future notes include the Liberty engines and drawings of the internal structures of the tail, wing, and pontoons of the various seaplanes he serviced.

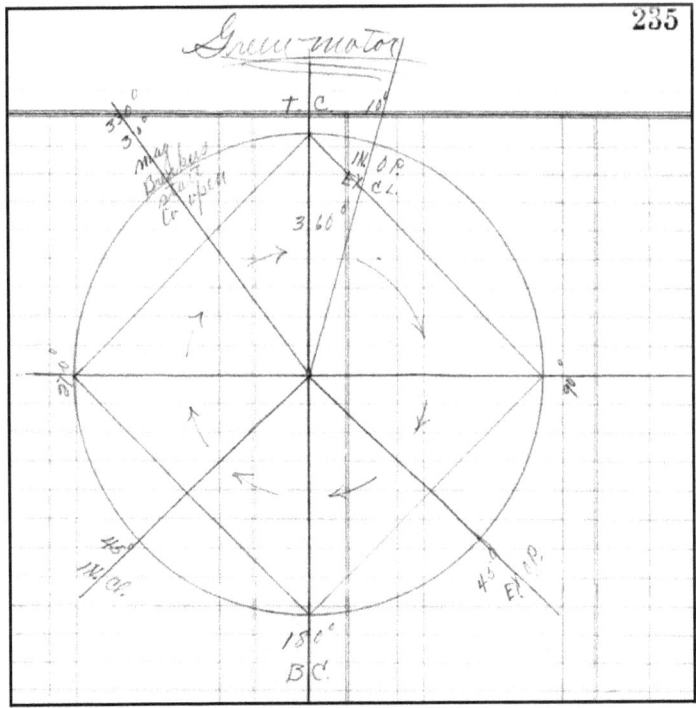

Arthur's diagram of Green Motor specs.

June 30, 1919
Monday
Got up at 6.45 A.M.
had breakfast
Got boat ready for
flight had lunch
made speed test from
Fort Mifflin to Hangar
for 2 hrs
    Gasoline throttles on
the bum one propeller
on the bum came down
took off propeller
went home had
dinner wrote letters
read newspaper
and went to bed at
9.30 P.M.

July 1, 1919
Tuesday
Got up at 6. A.M.
had breakfast
Went to work
Fixed propeller
put it on again
but new valve in
gass. line Fixed
throttles changed
carburettor off Starboard
motor quit work
at 4.15 P.M. had
dinner read newspaper
untill 8. P.M. Stella. B.
and Sister came at
8.30 took them home
at 12. A.M. Went to
bed at 1.30 AM

Fort Mifflin, PA is a famous Revolutionary War site located along the Delaware River.
Also called Mud Island, it is considered haunted by many.
(Courtesy of the National Park Service)

Arthur's crew with one of their seaplanes. Photography was banned in the Naval Aircraft Factory,
but Art took a few pictures and his landlord, Mr. Cushman, developed them privately.

July 2, 1919
Wednesday
Got up at 6 oclock
had breakfast
Went to work
Filled tanks with
gass (50 gall)
adjusted gass throttles
had lunch
Made speed test from
1.30 untill 4.39 P.M.
quite work at 4.45 P.M.
had dinner wrote
letters Went to bed
at 11. P.M.

July 3, 1919
Thursday
Got up at 4.30 A.M.
had breakfast
took both propellers
off & put on new
ones Got ready
for flight Went up
for Altitude test got
up to 5000 ft altitude
water got above 212°
had to come down
quite work at 8 oclock
had dinner read
books went to bed
at 11.30 P.M.

Liberty motor clearances.

	Diameter-End		Clearance	
	Min	Max	Min	Max
Crankshaft.	.0025	.0035	.0515	.0775
Connecting rods { forked.	.003	.004	.008	.020
plain end.	.005	.0065	.004	.008
Cam shaft.	.001	.003	.002	.014
Cam shaft upper drive shaft.	.0015	.0025	.002	.008
Rocker levers.	.0005	.00175	.005	.010
Water pump shaft.	.0015	.0035	.006	.010
" " Bevel driver.	.001	.0025	.065	.008
Oil pump gears in housing.	.001	.005	.002	.007
Piston pin { fit in rod.	.0025	.00125		
fit in piston	.0025	.0175 (top .003 mid .002 bot .002)		
Piston ring in grooves.	.00125	.003		
Piston in cylinder	.020	.035		
Valve stems in guide EXH.	.004	.0065		
INT.	.005	.0045		
tappet clearance EXH.	.019	.021		
INT.	.013	.016		
Breaker gap.	.010	.013		
Spark plug gap.	.015	.017		
Inlet valve spring tension	.021	.041	.030 Desired	
Exhaust " " "	given compressed to 145 lbs			
	a length of 3¼" — 23½ lbs			

Art's notes: Liberty Motor clearances.

LETTERS HOME FROM A WWI SEAPLANE TEST MECHANIC

The Delaware River Gap circa 1900.
(Courtesy of the Library of Congress's Prints and Photographs division)

> July 4, 1919
> Friday
> Got up at 8 A.M.
> had breakfast
> came home at 8.30
> received letter stating
> my friend Fred
> Eisemann got killed
> by explosion went to
> work at 10. P.M.
> got boat ready for
> flight went up at
> 11.30 to altitude of 6.500ft
> went to Delaware water
> gap stayed in air 3½
> hours quite work at
> 4 oclock stayed home
> read papers went to
> bed at 8 oclock

Spanish Influenza Wanes / US Seaplane First to Cross the Atlantic

July 4, 1919

Dear Mother:

Just received your letter and almost fell over when I heard Fred was killed. That sure was hard luck. Don't you know Fred was the best pal I ever had, and it sure is worrying me too. But I suppose it was his turn.

I was just coming home on a furlough with him and was figuring on having a very good time, but I suppose I'll have to go alone. There wasn't a fellow I cared more for than Fred—and I would have done anything in the world for him.

I wonder, did he keep his $10,000 insurance and to whom is it made out? What is Mr. Eisemann going to do about Fred's wife?

Say Mother, let me know what Fred's wife's address is if you can. I want to write her a few lines.

Well, let me know how Fred's Dad is making out. I'll be home in August.

Your heartbroken son,
A. Ehrke

Fred Eisemann.

> *July 5, 1919*
> *Saturday*
> *Got up at 8 o'clock*
> *had breakfast*
> *wrote letters*
> *went to work at*
> *11 A.M. quit work*
> *at 4 P.M. had dinner*
> *went to bed at 9:30*

243

Inspection of Green motor.

stem	Guide	Seats	Springs	Remarks
1 worn	fair	poor	O.K.	marked
1 worn-burnt	burnt	poor	weak	seat in valve replaced
3 worn .005	worn	poor	O.K.	replace
2 slightly worn	fair	poor	O.K.	machined
3 worn .0038	fair	must be reground	O.K.	replace
3 worn .005	fair	must be reground	O.K.	replace valve
4 slightly worn	fair	fair	O.K.	and guide
4 fair	fair	fair	O.K.	must be reground
5 fair	fair	fair must be	O.K.	O.K.
5 slightly worn	O.K.	reground	O.K.	O.K.
6 worn .003	fair	must be reground	O.K.	O.K.
6 O.K.	slightly worn	fair	O.K.	O.K.

Inspection of cyl, pistons, & rings

	surface	Round test	Clearance	Remarks
Cylinders	poor	.001		scored
Piston	fair	.003 top	.002 top .014 bot	
Rings	fair		.002 - .0025	
Cyl.	fair (good)	.003		clean
Pist.	fair (good)	O.K.	.011 - .016	
Rings	fair	O.K.	.02 in groove	
Cyl.	poor	.0135		scored, rings sprung
Pist.	fair	O.K.	.009 - .030	
Rings	fair	O.K.	.002 - .0025	
Cyl.	poor	.004		slightly scored
Pist.	fair	O.K.	.010 - .017	
Rings	fair	O.K.	.002 - .0025	
Cyl.	poor	.005		scored
Pist.	fair	O.K.	.013 - .014	
Rings	fair	O.K.	.001 - .001	worn

Art's notes: Green Motor Inspection specifications.

Art's photo of the seaplane he flew to Hampton Roads.

Art's seaplane with a rowboat attached piloted by one of his crew members.

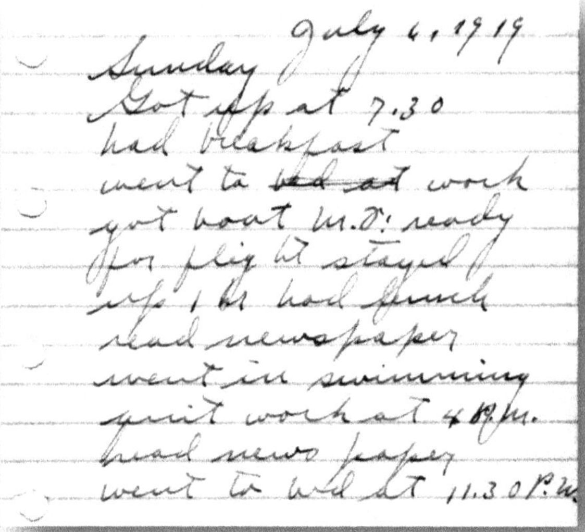

July 6, 1919
Sunday
Got up at 7.30
had breakfast
went to bed at work
got boat M.D. ready
for flight stayed
up, bt had lunch
read newspaper
went in swimming
quit work at 4 P.M.
read newspaper
went to bed at 11.30 P.M.

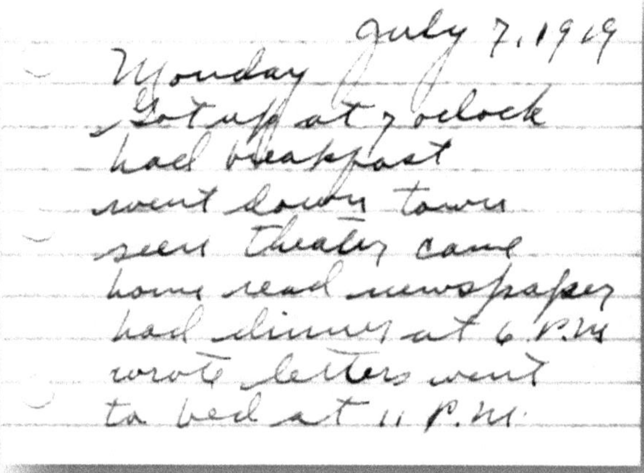

July 7, 1919
Monday
Got up at 7 o'clock
had breakfast
went down town
seen theater came
home read newspaper
had dinner at 6 P.M.
wrote letters went
to bed at 11 P.M.

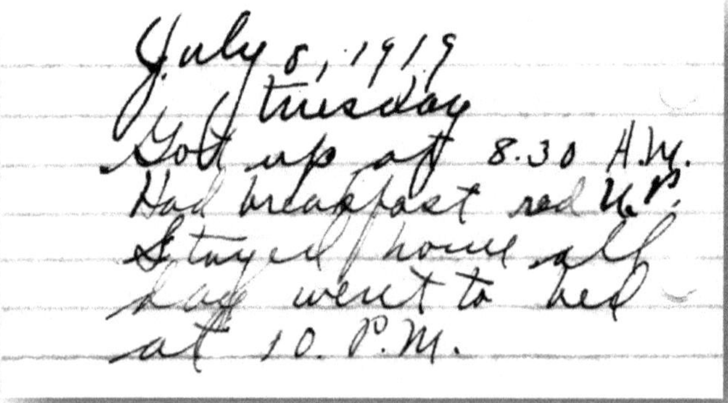

July 8, 1919
Tuesday
Got up at 8.30 A.M.
Had breakfast red up
Stayed home all
day went to bed
at 10 P.M.

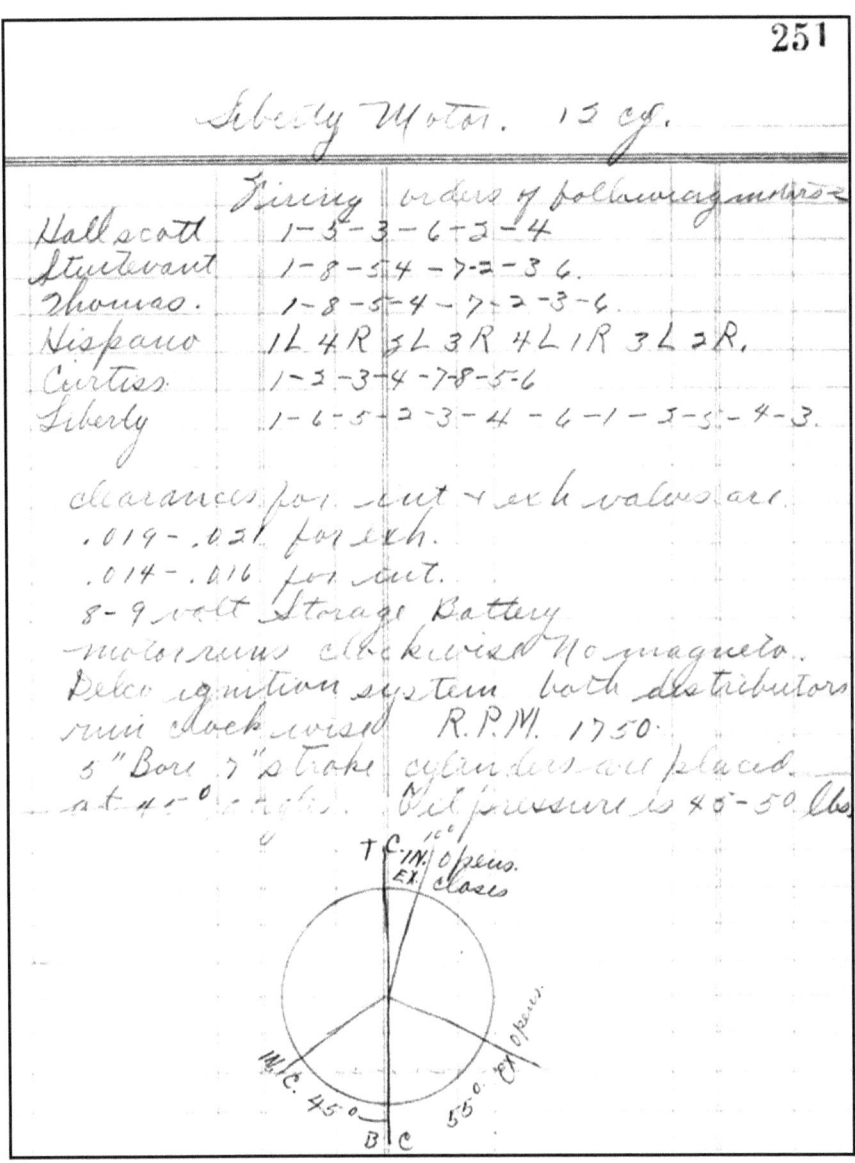

Firing orders of various motors.

252

Liberty engine.

Don't exhilerate to engine untill it has been run not less than 5 minutes at a speed not to exceed 500 R.P.M.

The following inst. should be carried out after every long run. Clean spark plugs, space each plug with .018" gauge. Remove front portion of magneto distributor and clean same, clean breaker points and just the two parrelel points to .014" and the third set of breaker points should be set at .012" Care should be taken that all wires running from mag. to be pushed to make good contacts these should be inspected daily. Care should be taken that the switch is not left on the on position while the motor is stopped as this won't stop discharge the battery.

Oil pressure should register about 45 to 55 lb. running at 1500 to 1700 R.P.M.

Lubrication oil recomended for this motor is mobile B. Oil all exposed moving parts oil all bearings before each run.

Valve clearance for int. is .014" to .015" and the exhaust jar in .019 to .021".

Oil should be drained from these motors every 5 hours running and crank case washed out with Kerosene and refilled with new oil.

Art's Liberty Engine notes.

> July 9, 1919
> Wednesday.
> Got up at 6.30 A.M.
> had breakfast
> Went to court martial
> room as witness
> for two Pilots
> quit work at
> 3 P.M. had dinner
> went out for walk
> with Jack Thomson
> borrowed car from
> Sofield returned
> car at 12.30 came
> home went to bed
> at 1.30 A.M.

Curtiss N-1 seaplane crash at the Philadelphia Naval Yards on June 29th, 1918.
(NH 43912—Courtesy of the Naval History and Heritage Command)

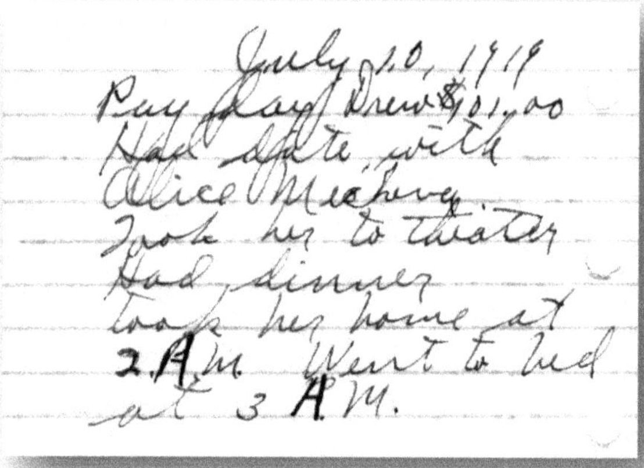

July 10, 1919
Pay day Drew $101.00
Had date with
Alice Michery.
Took her to theater
Had dinner
took her home at
2 A.M. Went to bed
at 3 A.M.

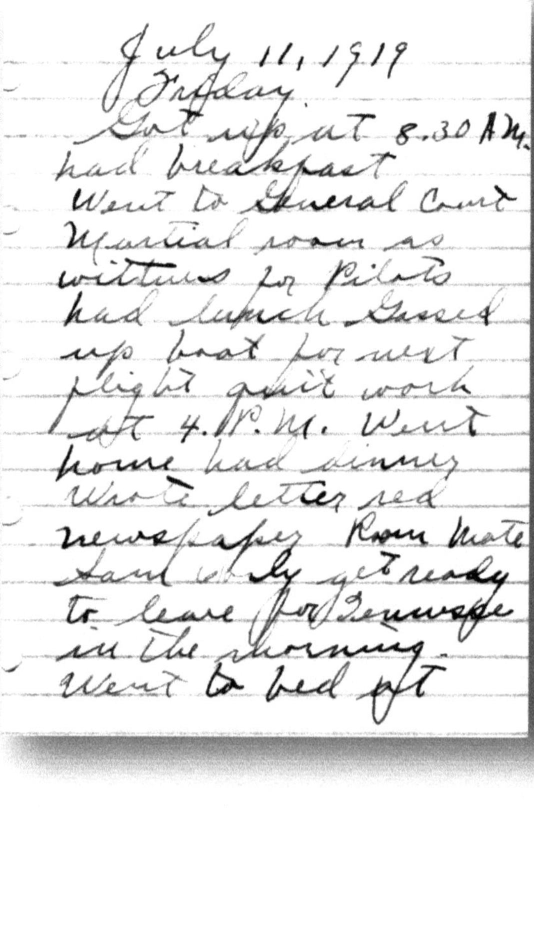

July 11, 1919
Friday
Got up at 8.30 A.M.
had breakfast
Went to General Court
Martial room as
witness for Pilots
had lunch Gassed
up boat for next
flight quit work
at 4. P.M. Went
home had dinner
Wrote letter read
newspaper Room Mate
Sam & I get ready
to leave for Bennwaspe
in the morning.
Went to bed ft

Naval Aircraft Factory, Philadelphia, PA, aerial view, 1918.
(NH 2664—Courtesy of the Naval History and Heritage Command)

```
                                              July 12, 1919

Miss Adele Ehrke
220 Wells Building
Milwaukee, Wisconsin

Dear Sister,

Just received your letter stating you would like to come
to Philadelphia. Well, you're welcome as the flowers in
Spring, and don't let anybody tell you different.

Now your fare will cost $29.22 one was without a berth
from home to here. Now you won't have to worry about any
cost while here, and I would gladly send you your fare
if I wasn't coming home this August. But I can't do
that.

Now take the C.M. & St. P. to Chicago. Then take the
Pennsylvania railroad (not the B.& O.) to Philadelphia.
```

You will have to change trains in Pittsburgh. Get off at Broad St. and Station.

"Let me know what train you are coming on, and I'll meet you. Listen, ask Mother why she don't write.

Your Brother,
Arthur.

Chicago, Milwaukee and Saint Paul Railway Station.
(Courtesy of *The Perry News*)

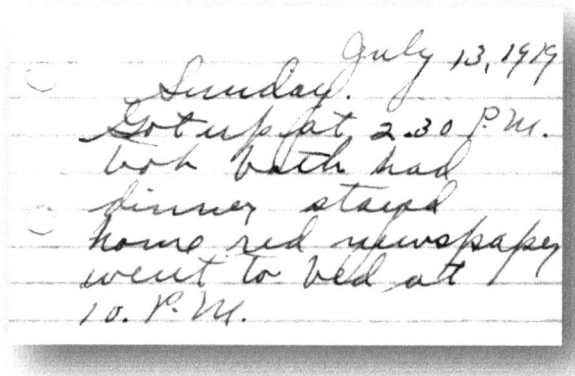

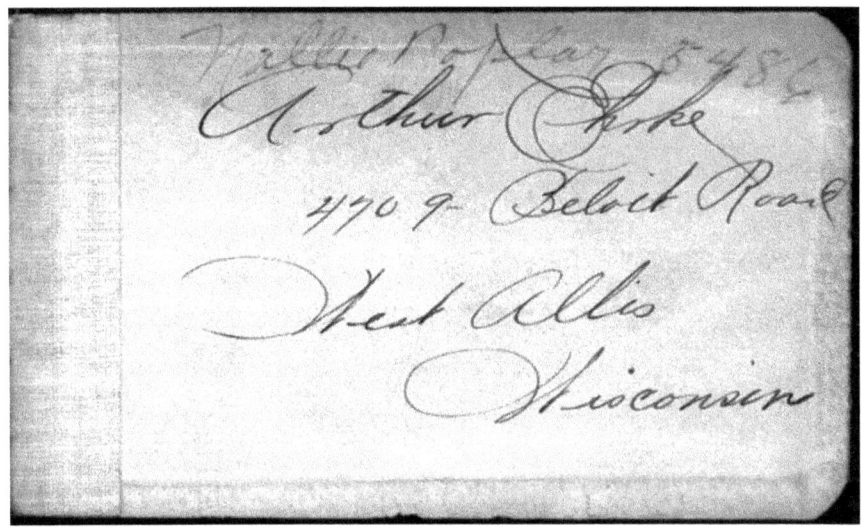

Arthur's signature and address in his notebook.

"If you ever find me dead" instructions.

Note from Arthur's sister Adele.

Letters Home from a WWI Seaplane Test Mechanic

> July 13, 1919
>
> Dear Mother,
>
> I haven't received a letter in about ten days. What's the matter? You said you would let me know how Fred's Dad made out,--but surely it did not take him ten days to go to Ohio, and you know I'm just dying for news about Fred.
>
> How is everything in West Allis? Same as usual I suppose. You remember I said I was coming home in August 10th? Well I might be out of the Navy by that time.
>
> The latest dope around here is that all Naval Reserve will be mustered out by August 7th. Now I don't know how right that is.
>
> My roommate is already mustered out of the Service. He leaves for Tennessee tomorrow morning. So, I'm out of luck again if I ain't mustered out by August 10th.
>
> I'll come home anyway, so you can expect me home around that time.
>
> Your son,
> A. Ehrke

Arthur (bow seat) with his crew before the crash.

Arthur's dog tags, keys, and pocket knife. His tags not only had his name printed on one side, but Art's fingerprint was emblazoned on the other side.

Arthur Ehrke died on July 14, 1919.

CARRY ON!

It's easy to fight when everything's right,
And you're mad with the trill and glory.
It's easy to cheer when victory's near,
And wallow in seas that are gory.
It's a different song when everything's wrong,
When you're feeling infernally mortal.
When it's ten against one, and hope there is none,
Buck up, little sailor, and chortle.
There are some who drift out in an ocean of doubt,
And some who in brutishness wallow,
There are others, I know, who in piety go,
Because of a Heaven to follow.
But to labor with zest and to give of your best,
For the sweetness and joy of the giving,
To help folks along with a hand and a song
Why, there's the real sunshine of living.
Carry on! Carry on!
Let the world be the better for you
And last when you die,
Let this be your cry—
Carry on, my soul, carry on!

Logbook of the Naval Aircraft Association 1917-1918

Chapter Five
Arthur Ehrke's Untimely Death

"In great deeds, something abides. On great fields, something stays. Forms change and pass; bodies disappear; but spirits linger, to consecrate ground for the vision-place of souls... generations that know us not and that we know not of, heart-drawn to see where and by whom great things were suffered and done for them, shall come to this deathless field, to ponder and dream; and lo! the shadow of a mighty presence shall wrap them in its bosom, and the power of the vision pass into their souls."
—Joshua Lawrence Chamberlain

A Navy seaplane crash with launch in the Delaware River circa 1918.
(Courtesy of the Fighting America Flying Boats of WWI Vol.2)

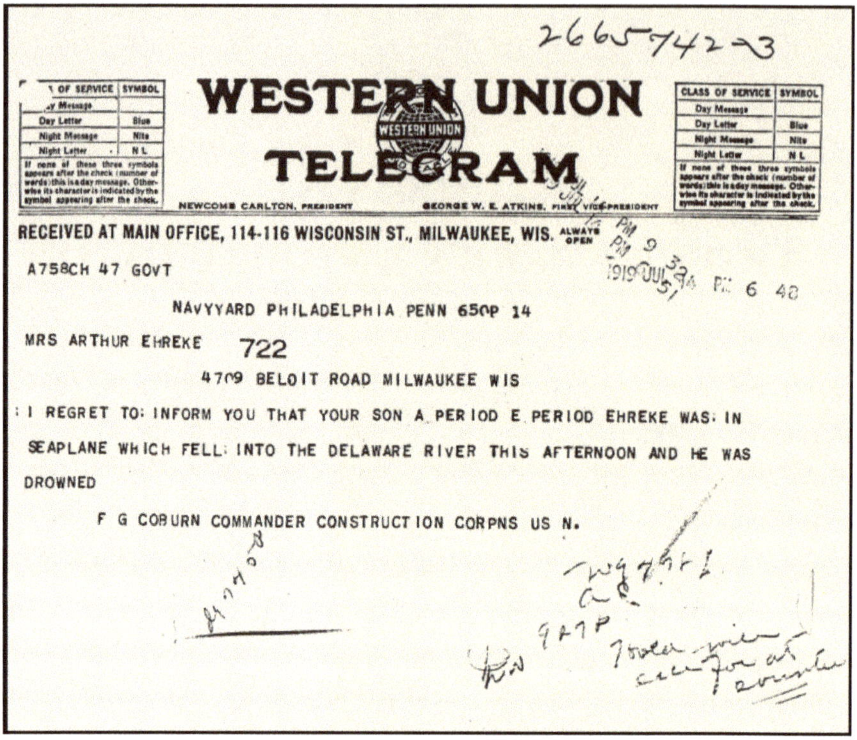

WESTERN UNION TELEGRAM

NEWCOMB CARLTON, PRESIDENT GEORGE W. E. ATKINS, FIRST VICE-PRESIDENT

RECEIVED AT MAIN OFFICE, 114-116 WISCONSIN ST., MILWAUKEE, WIS. ALWAYS OPEN

A758CH 47 GOVT

NAVYYARD PHILADELPHIA PENN 650P 14

MRS ARTHUR EHREKE 722

4709 BELOIT ROAD MILWAUKEE WIS

I REGRET TO INFORM YOU THAT YOUR SON A PERIOD E PERIOD EHREKE WAS IN SEAPLANE WHICH FELL INTO THE DELAWARE RIVER THIS AFTERNOON AND HE WAS DROWNED

F G COBURN COMMANDER CONSTRUCTION CORPNS US N.

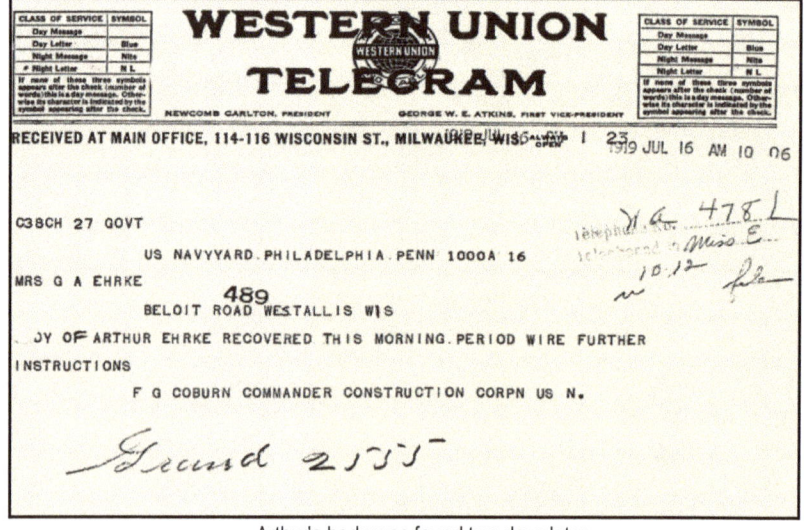

Commander Colburn's telegram informing Gustav and Mathilda Ehrke that their son's seaplane crashed and Arthur drowned on July 14th, 1919.

WESTERN UNION TELEGRAM

NEWCOMB CARLTON, PRESIDENT GEORGE W. E. ATKINS, FIRST VICE-PRESIDENT

RECEIVED AT MAIN OFFICE, 114-116 WISCONSIN ST., MILWAUKEE, WIS. ALWAYS OPEN 1919 JUL 16 AM 10 06

C38CH 27 GOVT

US NAVYYARD PHILADELPHIA PENN 1000A 16

MRS G A EHRKE 489

BELOIT ROAD WESTALLIS WIS

...DY OF ARTHUR EHRKE RECOVERED THIS MORNING PERIOD WIRE FURTHER INSTRUCTIONS

F G COBURN COMMANDER CONSTRUCTION CORPN US N.

Grand 2155

Arthur's body was found two days later.

LOCAL MAN KILLED AS AIRPLANE FALLS

July 14 1919

Son of Socialist Official Drowned as Craft Plunges.

Arthur Ehrke, oldest son of Gustave Ehrke, 4709 Beloit Rd., Socialist member of the West Allis fire and police commission, was one of three aviators drowned Sunday in the Delaware river, when a five passenger seaplane plunged into shallow water off the navy yard, Philadelphia, according to word received here Tuesday.

Ehrke was a chief machinists' mate and would have been 20 years old Sept. 17. He obtained his training for service in the aviation branch at the Philadelphia navy yard. In addition to his parents, he is survived by a brother, Walter, aged 7, and two sisters, Adela aged 21, and Lilian 15.

A life long chum of the young man, Fred Eisman, 704 47th Ave., West Allis, who enlisted the same day as Ehrke, May 27, 1918, was killed two weeks ago in a gas tank explosion in Akron, O.

The plane in which Ehrke met his death was making a test flight, and was about 200 yards above the water when it went down into the water, nose first and straight to the muddy bottom.

According to the father, arrangements have been made to bring the body to Milwaukee for burial as soon as it is recovered.

Milwaukee Journal graphic.

July 1919 *West Allis Star* article.

As you have seen, Arthur started a diary a month before he died. A man a few words, it took his passing away to reveal the more intimate details about his life. Hungry for more information about her son, Mathilda contacted the Cushman boarding house to learn more. Mr. and Mrs. Cushman had developed a deep relationship with Arthur and took the time to write three detailed letters, which provide riveting information about what happened on the fateful days before his passing. For example, on July 9th, July 11th, and again on July 14th, Arthur mentioned court martial hearings he attended in his diary. Apparently two pilots had been caught trying to test fly a seaplane while intoxicated. As the lead mechanic, Arthur was required to testify because he had prepared the plane. Fortunately, Mr. Cushman discovered the back story.

To provide historical context, the National Prohibition Act, known informally as the Volstead Act, prohibited all alcoholic beverages above 0.05% by volume was ratified by the states in January 1919 and officially went into effect the following January 1920. Originally designed to help redirect wheat from alcohol production to the war effort, Prohibition passed just as the Great War ended. When sobriety was mandated by federal law, every state started clamping down on all alcoholic beverages before the end of December 1919 deadline. And of course, the US Navy brass would investigate any pilots who had a record of being inebriated and crash-landing seaplanes in 1919.

Arthur testified at a court martial on the day he died because he had observed the pilots in question since he prepared and signed off their plane before take-off. The pilots later crash-landed their seaplane at Hampton Roads. Arthur didn't like these pilots because they were dare-devils, from his point of view.

Arthur was involved in several seaplane crashes where the pilots and crew members died, while others did not. He apparently came up with the idea that jumping into the water rather than staying in the plane was his best survival option under certain circumstances. Arthur chose to climb out on the wing and jump in the water before his seaplane crashed the day he died. Since the pilot and the crew member seated in front of the plane also died, everyone must have known a hard landing was coming.

As fate would have it, the Delaware River was shallow and mucky at the crash site. When Arthur jumped in the water to free himself from the plane, he implanted himself into river bottom muck. Unfortunately, he was unable to free himself and immediately drowned. That is the reason it took a couple of days to find Arthur. The family was advised by the U.S. Naval Hospital Commander to not open his casket. The final documents and correspondences about Arthur follow.

Arthur Ehrke's Untimely Death

Inventory of Arthur's effects on 7-16-19, which shipped on 8-7-19. The form they used was a deserter's inventory, which was blacked out to read "deceased."

Letters Home from a WWI Seaplane Test Mechanic

                        Milwaukee, Wis., July 16, 1919.

                        Arthur Ernest Ehrke,
                        Enlisted May 27, 1918.
                        Killed July 14, 1919.
                        Legal Island Navy Yards, Philadelphia, Pa.
                        Insurance Certificate No. 2947298.

Auditor for the War Department,
Washington, D. C.

Dear Sir:

      The above enlisted man died on or about July 14, 1919. I desire to apply for all arrears of pay and allowances due him from the United States. My relationship to him is that of father.

      I am his next of kin and I am informed that he left no will. Please send me the necessary application blank.

                        Yours very truly,

                        Gustav A. Ehrke
                        Gustav Ehrke
                        4709 Beloit Road,
                        West Allis, Wis.

[Stamp: DATE RECEIVED JUL 18 1919, For War Department, OFFICE OF AUDITOR]

Appendix 2 contains seventeen additional personal effects and compensation letters to and from various government agencies that this letter started. The last letter from the Veterans Administration awarded my grandparents $15 dollars a month compensation commencing June 14th, 1937.

Arthur Ehrke's Untimely Death

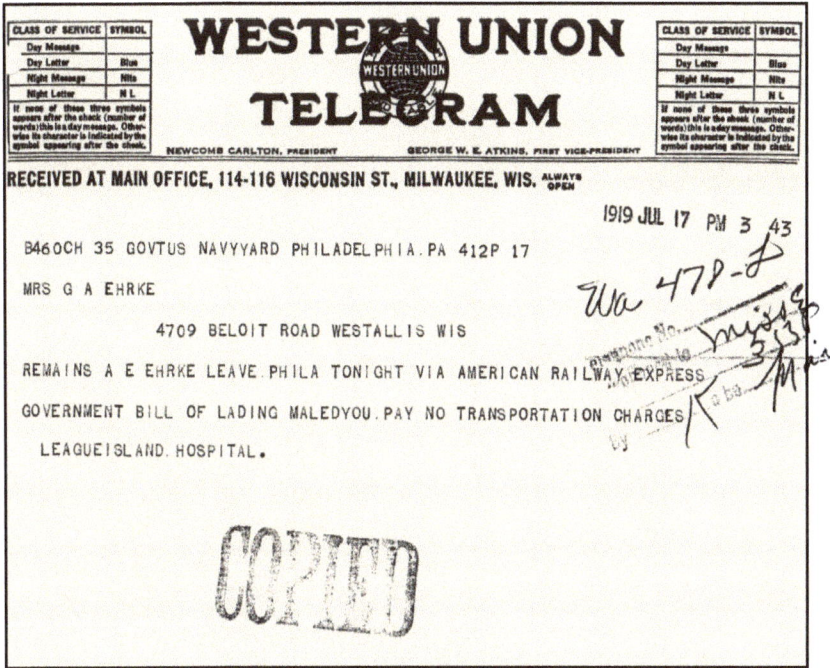

Western Union Telegram announcing that Arthur's remains were shipped, no transportation charges due.

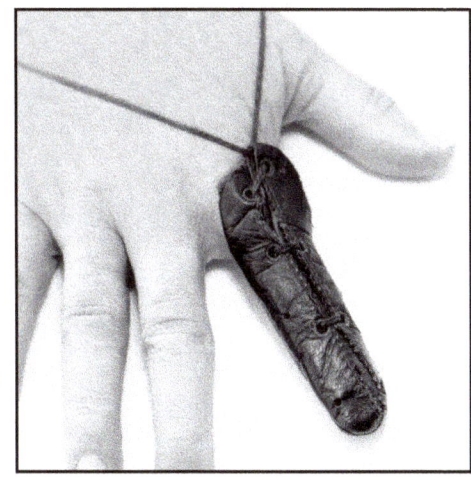

Art lost the tip of his finger while fixing a broken gasoline gauge, according to my mother. Here is the splint he crafted, which was returned with his belongings.

U. S. NAVAL HOSPITAL
League Island, Pa.

July 17th, 1919.

Mrs. G. A. Ehrke,
4709 Beloit Road,
West Allis, Wisconsin.

My dear Madam:—

The remains of your son are being forwarded tonight by American Express and there is enclosed herewith a Government Bill of Lading covering the shipment.

The body of your son has been embalmed and placed in our Navy Standard shipping case, as outlined in the circular enclosed. As the remains were in the water for nearly two days before they were recovered, I would strongly advise that the casket be not opened. Every effort has been made to prepare the body for shipment properly but the distressing circumstances in connection with your son's death, brought his body to us in such shape that we feel it necessary to give you the foregoing advice.

I desire to extend to you my sympathy on this occasion and to assure you of the sympathy of all of his acquaintances here.

Very sincerely yours,

R. C. Streemn

Commander (MC) U.S.N.
Commanding Hospital.

MTH

Warning from the Commander at the Commanding Hospital not to open the casket.

Chicago, July 17-1919

Mr & Mrs. Gustav Ehrke
   Milwaukee Wis.
Dear Aunt & Uncle & Cousins

Our sympathy is with you at this most sorrowful time. We regret deeply the untimely death of your son and our dear cousin Arthur.

We are doubly sorry that it is impossible for us to be at the burial.

In sorrow your
Niece & Nephew
Loretta & Harvey

Condolence letter.

N. M. S. 124677-1

INFORMATION FOR NEXT OF KIN

REGARDING EXPENSES IN CONNECTION WITH THE PREPARATION, ENCASEMENT, AND TRANSPORTATION OF THE REMAINS OF NAVAL DEAD

All expenses in connection with the preparation, embalming, clothing, and encasement of naval dead, and of transportation to such point as may be designated by the next of kin, are borne by the Government.

The remains are encased in the Navy standard shipping casket, designed to withstand shipment from the most distant parts of the world and to meet every requirement of the boards of health of foreign countries and of the different States. This casket is used alike for officers and enlisted men, no distinction being made for rank, and it is not customary to make transfer to a more elaborate casket.

Where the next of kin have been informed of the shipment of a body at Government expense, and, through some mistake, the transportation company endeavors to collect transportation charges, payment should be refused and a telegram sent immediately to the Surgeon General, Navy Department, Washington, D. C., collect, stating the circumstances.

After the remains have been delivered to the next of kin at the place designated by them, the Navy Department is unable to defray any of the expenses which may be incurred in connection with the funeral, interment, etc., there being specific law prohibiting such payment. The act of Congress approved October 6, 1917, however, provides for the payment by the United States of burial expenses not to exceed $100, under the jurisdiction of the Bureau of War-Risk Insurance, Treasury Department, Washington, D. C., with which office you should communicate.

All officers and enlisted men of the Navy are entitled to burial, with military honors, in the National Cemetery at Arlington, Va. (near Washington), or in any one of the naval cemeteries located at different naval stations throughout the country, and when such interment is made no expense whatever devolves upon the relatives of the deceased. The graves in these cemeteries are marked with suitable headstones and are perpetually kept in perfect condition.

4—2672

The Navy paid $100 of Arthur's burial expenses.
Gustav highlighted that information but choose to rent six limousines at his own expense.

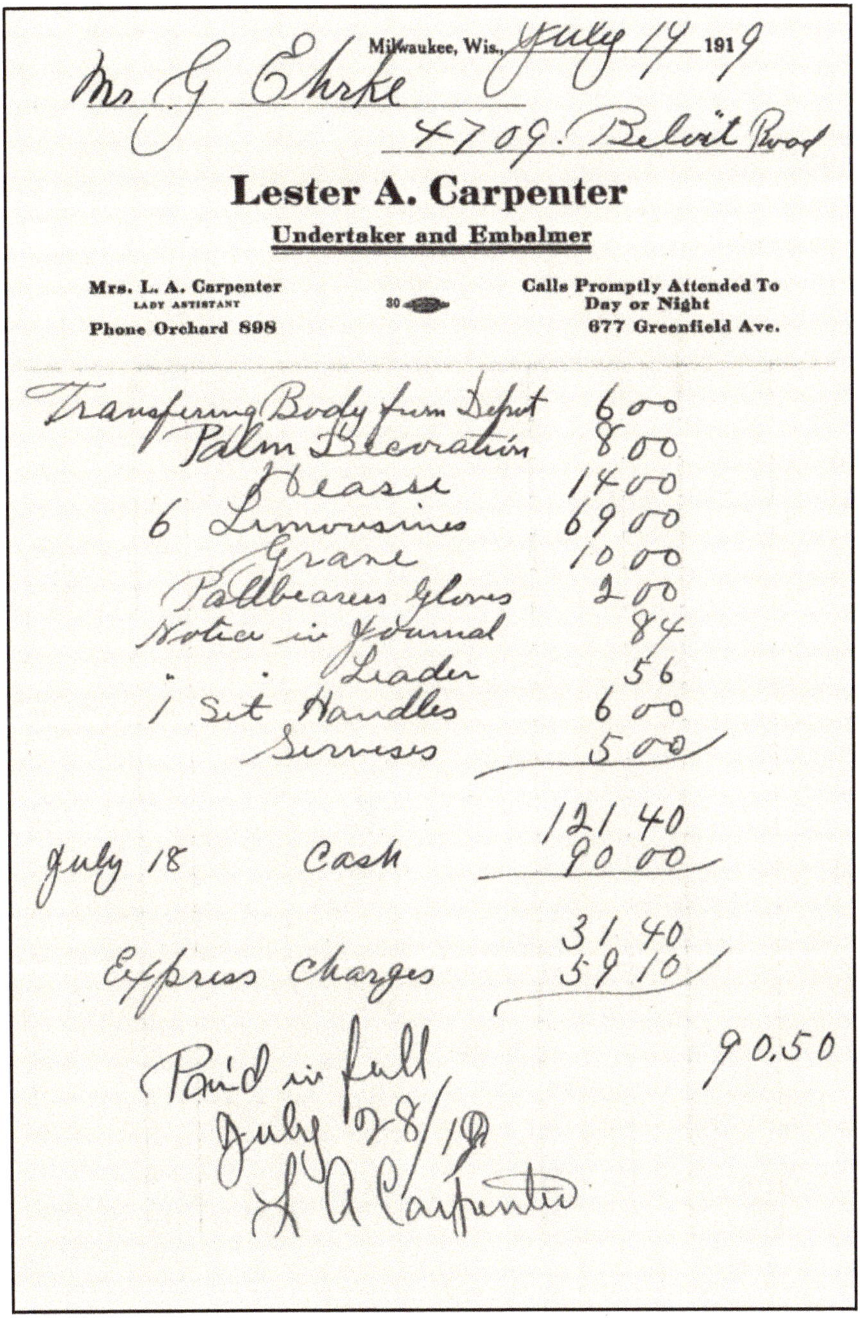

Milwaukee, Wis., July 14, 1919

Mr. G. Ehrke
4709 Beloit Road

Lester A. Carpenter
Undertaker and Embalmer

Mrs. L. A. Carpenter
LADY ASSISTANT
Phone Orchard 898

Calls Promptly Attended To
Day or Night
677 Greenfield Ave.

Transferring Body from Depot	6 00
Palm Decoration	8 00
Hearse	14 00
6 Limousines	69 00
Grave	10 00
Pallbearers Gloves	2 00
Notice in Journal	84
" " Leader	56
1 Set Handles	6 00
Services	5 00
	121 40
July 18 Cash	90 00
	31 40
Express charges	59 10
	90.50

Paid in full
July 28/19
L A Carpenter

Arthur's funeral expenses totaled $180.50.

Arthur's limousine and loved ones at the family home in West Allis, WI.

Mathilde Ehrke, Arthur's mother.

Arthur in his dress uniform.

> Cameron, Wis.,
> July 28, 1919.
>
> Dear Friends:—
> It gave me distress to hear that your son and brother died. May God comfort you, for I cannot. It is well with the boy.
> Very likely Herbert and I shall call on you in autumn.
>
> Regardingly,
>
> W. Motzkus.

Arthur Ehrke's family is one of the nine Gold Star families honored at the West Allis, Wisconsin Historical Society pictured above.
(Courtesy of the West Allis Historical Society)

                            1519 Green St.

                            Phila. Pa.

July 22, 1919

Dear Mr. and Mrs. Ehrke:

We are indeed grieved at your recent calamity. I have
no need to tell you dear folks how much it has affected
us.

It seems that it is like having one of our own family
taken away from us, as Arthur was one of our best boys,
and it will some time before we can ever get him off
our minds.

He was so cheerful and happy, and it was a pleasure to
be in his company,--which we often were.

We know well and feel what you have lost, what you are
suffering, and have yet to endure.

We will not, therefore, by useless condolences open
afresh the sluices of your grief, nor, although min-
gling our tears with yours, will we say a word where
words are vain. But that it is some comfort to us both,
that the time is not very distant at which we are to
deposit our sorrows and suffering bodies, and ascend in
essence to a joyful meeting with the friends we have
loved and lost, and whom we shall still love and never
lose again.

May God bless you and support you under your heavy
affliction.

                                    Mr. and Mrs. Cushman.

AMERICAN RED CROSS
SOUTHEASTERN PENNSYLVANIA CHAPTER
HOME SERVICE SECTION
MIDDLE DISTRICT
218 SOUTH NINETEENTH STREET, PHILADELPHIA, PA.

INTER-OFFICE LETTER

DATE July 25, 1919.

TO: Miss Anne J. Barker, Home Service Section, A.R.C., Milwaukee, Wis.

FROM: Mrs. Elizabeth T. Dawkins, District Superintendent

SUBJECT: Arthur Ernest Ehrke, League Island Navy Yard, Philadelphia, Pa.

1   Upon receipt of your letter of July 17, in reference to the above named man, we beg to state that we visited 1519 Green Street, his former rooming house and found that on July 17, an officer from the Navy Yard called at the house and obtained all his effects. Mrs. Kushman, who has charge of the house, stated at the time she took a list of all articles and had since written a letter to his mother, in which she enclosed the said list.

2   Mrs. Kushman had only the very best of references to give Mr. Ehrke and said that she had never had a young man in her house as fine as he was. He was considerate and had always spoken of his mother in the finest terms.

3   She said that she was quite sure that he had a presentiment that he would not live, as he had told her Sunday night when she had given him a piece of pie and a glass of milk, that it was probably the last he would ever get from her. She had tried to encourage him about his trip on the plane, but he stated this would be the third time he had taken the trip with the same officer and he felt they would never land safely.

4   Mrs. Kushman also stated that she and her husband had thought so much of the young man that they had closed up his room for ten days after his death and even now she could not bear to rent it to anyone else, as he had gone away on Monday morning so full of health and life, she did not think it possible he would never return.

5   We sincerely hope this is the information you desire.

MH/C

Elizabeth T. Dawkins
District Superintendent.

MILWAUKEE CHAPTER
128 GRAND AVE.
TELEPHONE GRAND 5193
MILWAUKEE, WIS.

July 29, 1919.

Mrs. Gustave Ehrke,
4709 Beloit Road,
West Allis,
Wis.

My dear Mrs. Ehrke:

    Enclosed is a letter that I received yesterday from the American Red Cross, Philadelphia, Pa., in answer to the letter that I wrote asking that a visit be made to your son's boarding house.

    I am very happy to have such a splendid report to send you, as I am sure that it will make you feel assured that all who knew your son must have loved him.

    I do hope that you are feeling better than when I last saw you. It is hard to lose ones son. I will be glad to have you come in and see me any time that you are downtown, and I assure you that I am most happy to assist you in any way possible.

Yours most sincerely,

Marie Brodwolf

Secretary West Allis
Home Service Section
American Red Cross.

B-W

Encl.

Answered on Aug. 11—1919

TREASURY DEPARTMENT
WASHINGTON

BUREAU OF
WAR RISK INSURANCE

IN REPLY REFER TO:
C - 265030.

Aug. 6, 1919.

Dear Madam:

You are requested to execute the enclosed form pertaining to the benefits payable under the War Risk Insurance Act of October 6, 1917. You are advised that action is being taken to ascertain to whom Compensation and Insurance, if any, are payable in this case.

Compensation and insurance as referred to are separate and distinct Compensation is payable only to the widow, children, dependent mother, and dependent father of the deceased, provided death was the result of injury received or disease contracted in the line of duty. If death occurred in the service and expense was incurred for the return home and burial of the body an amount not exceeding $100 is payable by the War Risk Bureau in reimbursement.

Insurance validly applied for by the deceased is payable in monthly installments to his wife, child, grandchild, parent, brother or sister, whichever was named as beneficiary in his application, provided the insurance has been kept in force by the payment of the required monthly premiums. No dependency need be proven by a beneficiary of Insurance.

Inquiries concerning arrears of pay, personal effects and Liberty Bonds should be addressed as follows:

ARMY. Inquiries concerning back pay, personal effects should be addressed to the Auditor for the War Department, Washington, D. C., and those concerning Liberty Bonds to the Officer in charge of Liberty Bonds, Zone Finance Office, Washington, D. C.

NAVY. Inquiries concerning back pay, personal effects and Liberty Bonds should be addressed to the Auditor for the Navy Department, Washington, D. C.

MARINE CORPS. Inquiries concerning back pay, personal effects and Liberty Bonds should be addressed to the Paymaster, United States Marine Corps, Washington, D. C.

COAST GUARD. Inquiries concerning back pay, personal effects and Liberty Bonds should be addressed to the Captain Commandant, United States Coast Guard, Washington, D. C.

All future correspondence in this case should bear the deceased's full name and the file number C- 265030.

Very truly yours,
R. H. Hallett,
~~JOHN W. BARTON~~
Assistant Director, in charge of
Compensation and Insurance Claims Division.

jbc

Form C. C. 564

Letters Home from a WWI Seaplane Test Mechanic

August 15, 1919

Dear Mr. and Mrs. Cushman:

We received your letter July 26th, and was very glad to hear from you. I answered your letter July 31st, and have not received an answer. Would you please let me know if you received my letter, or did it get lost, or were you unable to write? I am very anxious to know.

You are the only one we can write to—we don't know any of his friend's addresses. I wrote to one of his friends in the hospital,--R.R. Warmer, but I did not receive an answer from him. Won't you please be so kind and let me know his address so I could write to him.

Dear Mrs. Cushman, I must thank you again for being so good to my boy, Arthur, the last day when you gave him a piece of pie and a glass of milk, and those kind words you spoke to him when he went on his last trip. Dear Mrs. Cushman in the Red Cross letter it says that Arthur always spoke of his Mother. Won't you please let me know what his last words were? Didn't he say anything about his home or his Mother? OH! How I miss Arthur every time the mail man passes. We think we must get a letter from Arthur, --but he won't write anymore.

Won't you please write a few words to us and let us know how the accident happened. We don't know anything—only what was in the paper—it said that the plane came down in the Delaware River. Was there anything broken that they could not get out? And did they find the other two Aviators? I hope they find them. It must have been awful to see the plane come down and no way to help them.

Dear Mrs. Cushman in the last letter I wrote to you all about Arthur's funeral and the pretty flower pieces he had. If you didn't get my letter, I will let you know all about it next time.

I will have to close now, please excuse my writing. Hoping to hear from you soon. If I am not asking too much, please write at your earliest convenience.

Yours Sincerely,
Mr. and Mrs. G. Ehrke

Mathilda Pawelke and Gustav Ehrke's wedding, Sept. 18, 1897.

Mathilda, Della, and Gustav Ehrke circa 1898.

Letters Home from a WWI Seaplane Test Mechanic

1519 Green St.
Phila. Pa.

Aug. 21, 1919

Dear Mr. and Mrs. Ehrke,

We have received both of your letters. In fact, the second one we have just finished reading and was very pleased to hear from you. Why we did not answer your first letter before, was on account of our being away on a little vacation at the sea-shore.

But next time will try and be a little more prompt in answering your letters. But we have quite a few to answer now, seeing that quite a few of the boys who were with us and are being mustered out of the service. Arthur's roommate, Mr. Jolly was sent to Atlanta, Georgia to be mustered out the Saturday before Arthur's death, so of course we have just received a letter from him asking us all about the fatality which happened in the Navy Yard, as he had only heard a very little about the same, I suppose as you did. For he did not know who was in the plane as the paper in his home town did not state it.

So, I think he may consider himself very lucky as to be fortunate enough to have received his papers in time to be mustered out. If I am not mistaken, I think one of the boys told me Arthur's discharge was laying on the desk at the Navy Yard ready to have them take action on is discharge, but I am not quite sure whether it was right or not.

The last time we saw Arthur was on the Sunday night before the accident and we were all sitting out in front of the house talking together, but he did not seem as cheerful as we generally found him. So my wife asked what was the matter, and he says he has to go up tomorrow with a machine and the pilot he did not like to, as he was one of them dare-devils, so we think he must have felt as though something was going to happen to him.

We have seen and talked with quite a few of the boys from the Yard, and they tell us if Arthur had stayed in the machine, he might have come out all right, as where

Arthur Ehrke's Untimely Death

he rode in the machine, there was another fellow with him, and this fellow came out of the accident without a scratch. But Arthur told us that if anything was to happen that he was going to be where he could jump, so it seems by what this fellow says that just as soon as they saw the plane was in trouble, that Arthur climbed out on the wing of the machine and that was the last he saw of him. Warmer, the boy who was saved with only a few cuts and a broken leg was sitting alongside of the Pilot who was killed, and the other man who was in the front of the machine was killed also.

I happened to be working on the opposite shore and saw the machine crash into the water, but did not know at the time who was killed, as I did not hear no more till I came home that evening, and of course when I heard of Arthur's death, why I was very much upset.

We then tried to find out as much as we could about it ourselves, but you know, they would not give us any information to speak of. It is also very hard to get into the Yard unless you are

Page 2
Aug. 21, 1919

employed there. So for that reason we did not hear the full particulars till the following morning, and of course then we heard that only one of the bodies had been recovered—that being Souder. And of course in the meantime, they were still hunting for Arthur's and the Pilot's bodies. I think Arthur's body was the last to be recovered. Just as quick as they found the bodies, why one of the Officers from the Navy Yard came to house and got all of Arthur's belongings. We did not want to give them up at first on account of we thought we would hear from you as to what to do, but he stated that Arthur was still under the care of the U.S. Government and they had charge of him even though he lived outside the Yard.

So to have everything straight and not have any trouble we had him make a list of everything, and we also kept a list of which I am sending you. Of course we do not know what he had in his locker at the Yard, but the Chief Officer told us he took are of all them things.

In regard to the ring which you mention in your letter I cannot say whether he had it on or not, as we very seldom saw him in the morning as he did not eat with us, but took his meals outside. The last we saw of Arthur, as I have written a few lines back was on Sunday evening. Now Mrs. Ehrke in regards to Liberty Bonds, will say the Postman was here today and as near as he can tell us, I think he has them as he wanted Arthur and also Mr. Jolly. But of course we had to tell him where to send Mr. Jolly's and Arthur's. So I think you will be hearing something in a few days in regards to same. We gave him your address.

We feel very sorry that we could not have had one more look at Arthur ourselves, but only one or two boys who worked at the Yard saw him. I was talking to one of the boys this evening and he says Mr. Warmer is coming along nicely, and I told him to tell Warmer that you would like to hear from him. I have also given your address to one of Arthur's friends who is a C.P.O. (Chief Petty Officer) the same as Arthur, and he says he will write you.

Arthur's Chief Officer was a Mr. West who is a very fine man and whom Arthur thought a great deal of. In fact, Arthur was a boy, if he once liked a person he could not do any too much for them, and I know that everyone who came into contact with him, also spoke highly of him.

Saturday evening he was only telling how he expected his Sister to see him and how she had written to him about coming on and stopping at the Y.W.C.A. #1800 Arch which is only 5 blocks away from us, and I know he was so pleased for he had been to the Broad St. Station on Saturday evening and got time-tables of the different trains which came in from Chicago.

He also spoke quite a good deal about his home and about his friend who was killed in Akron, Ohio. In fact, I think Arthur took that to heart quite a good deal, for he would often say to the wife that he certainly did lose his best friend when you wrote and told him about his death.

Arthur Ehrke's Untimely Death

Page 3
Aug. 21, 1919

Most all the boys who were in the service with Arthur's crew have all been mustered out, and of course we do get to hear much about the Navy Yard. I believe there are only three left now who have enlisted over for another four years. They are a Mr. West, and Adrian who are Chief Petty Officers and a sailor by the name of Owens and Warmer, who of course is still in the League Island Hospital. If you care to have their address, why most any letter would reach them, addressing their name in care of the Aeroplane Hanger, League Island, Navy Yard, Phila. Pa.

I really don't know whether Arthur had sent you a photograph of himself or not, but the one that I thought so much of and one which I prize I was unable to get enlarged. There was something wrong in my developing the films and they could not make an enlargement from it. But just as quick as I can, I will send you a few photos which I have taken now and then. If I am not mistaken, there were quite a few pictures which we took off the looking glass in Arthur's room and sent in a box.

The one where you see a man standing on the wing with glasses is the Mr. Parker who was on the fatal trip and who was right beside Arthur, he was saved without receiving a scratch. Most all of the other pictures are scenes of the League Island Navy Yard and vicinity taken from the aeroplane. You know they were not allowed to have a camera inside the Yard, but they often used to take Jolly's Kodak down and then bring them home for me to develop.

Mrs. Ehrke, the last words we can remember of Arthur saying was in case anything should happen to him was to notify you—or the way he put it was to notify my mother. But of course we did not, for just as quick as we were in touch with the Navy Yard by phone they told us that they would tend to everything, so that is why you did not hear from us.

We will always be pleased to hear from you people and am sorry that we are not closer so as we could call upon one another. But if anytime any of your folks should happen to reach this vicinity, we shall be pleased to have you call and see us.

Respectfully yours,
Mr. and Mrs. Cushman

P.S. Am sending a clipping which I have carried in my pocket so forget the dirty appearance.

Mr. Parker survived the crash.

ARTHUR EHRKE'S UNTIMELY DEATH

TREASURY DEPARTMENT

WASHINGTON

BUREAU OF
WAR RISK INSURANCE

C265030

8/21/19

Mr. Gustave G̶e̶o̶r̶g̶e̶ Ehrke,

Dear Sir: You are hereby notified that you were named as a beneficiary of insurance in the amount of $10,000 issued by the United States Government to your son, Arthur Ernest Ehrke,

___Chief Mechanic, League Island /Navy Yards.___
Rank or rating   Organization, station or vessel

who died on the fourteenth day of July 1919.

Enclosed you will find a blank form of affidavit which you will kindly fill in, and execute before a notary public, commissioner of deeds or any other person authorized by law to administer an oath and return the same to this Bureau in the enclosed envelope which needs no postage.

Your signature must be witnessed by two persons who must sign their names and affix their addresses in the place provided for the same on the affidavit. You will note at the bottom of the affidavit the penalty as provided by the Act of October 6, 1917.

In the event the beneficiary named is a minor, a guardian must be appointed to receive the insurance payments. A certified copy of the guardianship papers must accompany this affidavit of beneficiary.

By authority of the Director:

R. H. HALLETT, Ass't Director.
In charge of C̶h̶i̶e̶f̶,
Compensation and Claims Division.

RB

Form 555

This is the only notification I received besides a telegram stating that he was killed July 14 - 1919.

G. A. Ehrke

Notice from the Treasury Department that Gustav was named Art's beneficiary. Problems occurred because Arthur had lied about his age, but they eventually paid.

Letters Home from a WWI Seaplane Test Mechanic

1519 Green St.
Phila. Pa.

Oct. 7, 1919

Dear Mr. and Mrs. Ehrke,

Your letter received some time ago, but am very sorry that I was unable to answer it until this time. As you know we have a lot a letters to answer as lots of the boys have been mustered out of the Army and Navy, and of course when they get home they write us and they always want an answer. So between that and my work and the work which takes up a good deal of our time here at the house, we are very busy. My wife is so busy here with the care of the house she cannot hardly find time to do anything else, so that is why I have to sit down and answer some of her letters.

And I have been having a very hard cold for the last few days which has made me feel very miserable. You asked us in your last letter if we had any pictures of Arthur. Well we have and I have tried to have one of them enlarged but the film was so bad that they cannot make an enlargement from it, but I don't see why they cannot as it prints a very nice small one which I will send you. And just as quick as I can, I will get my films together and make you a few more of different ones which I had taken at different times.

Page 2
Oct. 7, 1919

You see I did have quite a few, but some of the boys who were Arthur's friends wanted some, so I gave most of them away. But I will get right at it shortly and have more time to make them right, and will send you some.

In regards to the letter that you wrote about if Arthur had received it will say that it came Monday morning— and of course we don't receive the mail till around 9 o'clock so Arthur was at the Island, but it was put in his room as we do all mail, and then they get it when they come home. But very unfortunately that was the day of the mishap, so Arthur never saw the letter. But just as soon as we heard of the mishap, why my wife was worried and she opened it for she saw it was from Milwaukee, so she didn't know but it was from your daughter in regards to her coming on. So we thought she might have started and was her way here, as Arthur said she was to come that week. So my wife opened the letter to make sure of finding out if she had started or was on her way, or we didn't know but she might have come in that evening.

As near as we can find out from the boys, the Court martial which Arthur was a witness at was two pilots who came from Hampton Roads to take two machines from the Island back to Hampton Roads, and it seems that they came into the Yard intoxicated and wanted to take the machines up that day, but the Supt. would not let them go up. So they came back the next day and if course the testing crews had to go up with them for a little spin before they are sent away from the Island. Well, Arthur and his crew went up in one machine, and Stafford and his men in the other. So when they came back from their trial rip, they said everything was O.K.

But it seems that after these pilots had landed at Hampton Roads that they made a very bad landing and had smashed a few things on the planes, so the Admiral at Hampton Roads had reported it to Headquarters and wanted to find out if these two fellows had had liquor on the planes—as they were all right when they left Phila. So the Court Martial was held here at the Navy Yard—on account of this is where the start was made from. So the day that Arthur was killed, why they had had these two pilots here to find out where they got the liquor from. But neither crew on the trial trip around the Island had seen any liquor on the planes. The only thing they saw were the two suitcases which they saw the pilots put on the boats after they had started for Hampton Roads.

So of course they did not find anything against these fellows—for no one knows anything what they did after they left the Navy Yard. But while the crews were with them on the trial trip there wasn't any sign of liquor. But as they all think here at the Yard, they must have taken it on when they started for Hampton Roads. Of course that is something the Court never did prove, and they didn't even after they arrived at the Roads. So they either got it in Virginia unseen, or threw off the cases enroute . But they were never Court Martialed.

We do not see much of the boys who are still in the service now, as they have been taken off of subsistence, and are now at the Navy Yard all together, so the only time we do see one, is when

Page 3
Oct. 7, 1919

they are on a liberty day. In fact, there are only three left who we know, and it is very seldom we see them.

We had a letter from one of Arthur's friends who was mustered out and who had gone home and he, I guess, had not heard of the death of Arthur for he wanted to be remembered to him in his letter. You see they came from all over the United States—1 from Tenn., 2 from Texas, and 2 from New York.

Most of all the planes are being sent to Hampton Roads now to be tested. They just crate them up and send them by freight where before they were tested here and then pilots came here and flew them to the Roads.

Well, as this letter leaves us in very nice health, and hope it will find you and all of your family in good spirits, we will remain your friends.

Mr. & Mrs. Cushman

P.S. We will be pleased to hear from you at anytime and will try and write you as often. Hoping that your good spirits may keep up for the future.

Arthur Ernst Ehrke

A photo of Art in his backyard sent by the Cushmans.

TREASURY DEPARTMENT

BUREAU OF
WAR RISK INSURANCE

WASHINGTON Oct. 22, 1919.
Ehrke, Arthur Ernest
I-124513
C-265030
Navy

IN REPLY REFER TO:
JH/eh 12

Mr. Gustave A. Ehrke,
4709 Beloit Road,
Allie, Wis.

Sir:

    Acknowledgment is made of receipt of your letter stating that you have not received payment for July and August, 1919 on the above insurance award.

    In reply you are advised that check #1341764 in the amount of $89.03, representing payment from July 15, 1919 to August 31, 1919, has been mailed to you at the above address and has not been returned as unclaimed.

    If you have not yet received this check, it is suggested that you communicate with the local postal authorities, and if this does not result satisfactorily, write to the Division of Receipts and Disbursements, Bureau of War Risk Insurance, Washington, D.C., and request a form of Indemnity Bond to be used in case of lost checks.

    By authority of the Director:

R H Hallett
Assistant Director, in charge of
Compensation and Insurance
Claims Division.

Arthur's decision to buy the $10,000 War Risk Insurance was very helpful to my grandparents. Eventually, everything was straightened out.

Letters Home from a WWI Seaplane Test Mechanic

```
GEO. F. HAMBRECHT, CHAIRMAN              OF              STEWART SCRIMSHAW,
FRED M. WILCOX                                           SUPERVISOR OF APPRENTICESHIP
THOMAS F. KONOP                      WISCONSIN           CHARLES E. ESLINGER,
E. E. WITTE, SECRETARY                                       ASSISTANT SUPERVISOR

                            STATE CAPITOL, MADISON
                                              November 25, 1919.


        Mr. Gustav Ehrke,
        4709 Beloit Road,
        West Allis, Wis.

        Dear Sir:
                  We were recently informed that your son, Arthur,
        who was an apprentice with the Kempsmith Mfg.Company, had been
        killed in an aeroplane accident while in the service. We are
        indeed very sorry to learn of your loss. May we ask you to
        advise us the date of his death so that we may have our
        records complete?

                  Thanking you for this advice, and with deepest
        sympathy, I am

                              Very truly yours,

                              Stewart Scrimshaw
        S/B.                  Supervisor of Apprenticeship.
```

April 26, 1920

Dear Mr. and Mrs. Ehrke:

Just received your kind and welcome letter at hand and was more than glad to hear from you. I am very glad that I got your address as I have a white Sailor blouse that Arthur used to wear when he was a Sailor, and he said to me one afternoon that he ought to send his sister a white blouse. So I have one that belongs to Arthur, and his name is stamped on it, and I hope you will get it.

Well, Mrs. Ehrke, I was with Arthur the Sunday before he got killed. He was one good boy, and I thought a lot of him. I roomed with him about 7 or 8 months, and was with him a lot.

I was in the room the Sunday morning before he got killed when he got a Special Delivery letter from his Sister saying she was coming the next Saturday, and told him to go to the YWCA and engage a room for her.

> And I also got him up to go to work on the Monday morning before he got killed. I had just gotten out of the Navy about two weeks and had been down home in old Virginia and had just gone back to Phili. Pa. and that same Monday I went down to the Navy Yard about 12 o'clock and went down to the air station to see Arthur and he was out on the River getting the Sea Plane ready to make flight. So I could not get to see him then, and I went back to town, and about 4 p.m. I heard that his seaplane had fallen.
>
> Well, Mr. and Mrs. Ehrke, I don't know when I will ever be in Milwaukee, Wi., but if I am ever there, I will surely come up to see you.
>
> I have been working in the State of Texas, and my home is Gretna, Va. I will close, hoping to hear from you some time.
>
> Your friend,
R.A. Franklin
Hot Springs, Ark.

R.A. Franklin's letter is the last condolences my Aunt Dell saved as a memorial to her beloved brother. There are many other official documents where the War department responded to my grandparents' requests for back pay with bureaucratic officials. These letters and documents are located in Appendix 2. My personal thoughts and reflections about my uncle and family, when the written word held all our wishes, hopes, dreams and sorrow follow in the next chapter. The *Logbook of the Naval Aircraft Association 1917-1918* was written just after WWI ended. So, there are many references about endings because the comraderies everyone enjoyed were about to end due to peacetime demobilization.

THE LONG, LONG TRAIL

*There's a long, long trail a-winding
Into the land of my dreams,
Where the nightingales are singing
And a white moon beams.
There's a long, long night of waiting
Until my dreams all come true;
Till the day when I'll be going down
That Aircraft trail with you.*

Logbook of the Naval Aircraft Association 1917-1918

Arthur Ehrke (1899–1919).

CHAPTER SIX
PERSPECTIVES
AND OBSERVATIONS

A total of 122 naval aviators died overseas in combat during WWI and 86 died at home flying seaplanes, according to Capt. W. H. Sitz, in his book, *A History of Naval Aviation*. Arthur Ehrke witnessed others die before he became one of the fallen himself. During the war, seaplanes were easy targets for German U-boats. Most were shot down, which was why the US Navy hastily built and experimented with more effective seaplanes at the Naval Aircraft Factory. During the Great War, 431 Navy personnel were killed due to enemy action and 819 were wounded.

However, 5,027 Navy personal died as a result of the Spanish Influenza epidemic between the fall of 1918 and the spring of 1919, more deaths than at Pearl Harbor, Guadalcanal, or Okinawa. Nearly a fourth of the US population became infected by the pandemic and 675,000 people perished, to add to the 50 million who died worldwide. The Spanish Influenza helped end the war and unfortunately added to the collective suffering that writers at the time termed WWI's "Lost Generation." (*H-022-1: The Worst Killer of All—The Spanish Influenza, 1918-1919.*)

After the Armistice on November 11th, 1918, the Naval Aircraft Factory's mission immediately changed. By the end of the war, they produced one seaplane a day, but demobilization was about to reduce their workforce to 1,000 workers in the months ahead. So, the navy brass decided to create the *Logbook of the Naval Aircraft Factory 1917-1918* to honor everyone who worked there. Its dedication read:

> Navy Yard
> **NAVAL AIRCRAFT FACTORY**
> Philadelphia, Pa.
>
> **Office of the Manager**
>   22 November, 1918.
>
> **TO THE MEN AND WOMEN OF THE
> NAVAL AIRCRAFT FACTORY**
>
> WITH the ending of the war comes the end of our war mission, the large-scale production of aircraft; and there begins the peaceful mission of developing the art of flying.
>
> With this change of mission comes a readjustment of work involving the demobilization of a large part of our force; and this message is to those of us who are about to resume their peace-time activities.
>
> In August, 1917, the site of the Naval Aircraft Factory was a vacant lot. On it today are buildings and other equipment costing nearly $5,000,000, housing 3700 workers, and receiving for assembly the output of more than 7000 other workers in feeder plants. The factory has produced a large number of planes, and since it came into production has met all demands for output.
>
> This result was attained because all those who have been associated in the work have been loyal, patriotic, thorough Americans, who have co-operated and produced despite all the vexatious delays and impedances that have obstructed us.
>
> Our joy and thanksgiving due to the ending of the war and the accomplishment of our mission are tempered by the thoughts of breaking up and parting. We shall not all be together again, except in spirit; but in spirit we shall always be together, in the future as in the past, bound by the recollections of our labors, our trials, and our success.
>
>   F. G. COBURN,
>   Commander, Construction Corps, U. S. Navy,
>   Manager.

Dedicated to Those Men and Women Who Went—First and Last—and Going, Went with Smiles and Song, to Buy with their Sufferings or Their Lives our Freedom to be Joyful—a Little Longer.

F. G. Colburn, the commanding officer who sent the telegrams to my grandparents informing them of Arthur's death, wrote the open letter shown above to all personnel after Armistice Day.

Penned as a souvenir, the *Logbook* identified and photographed each department and provided a heartfelt glimpse of the comraderies enjoyed by the 3,700 people who worked there during the war, of which, nearly 1,000 were women. Like every man in the service, the women came from all walks of life. John McClure, the author of the *Logbook* stated, "their work is a factor in practically every department." He added the following paragraph about women working alongside men at the Naval Aircraft Factory on page 87:

> *"The men were grouchy about the women working, but the women did not merely do good work, but the finest quality of work. It was amazing to see them handle planes and hammers, and paint brushes. One high school girl was a master of the art of painting—a lovely girl too."*

This was a remarkable observation in 1919, since the women had to learn how to build a seaplane from scratch just like every man next to them. When the men went off to war, women had to fill the jobs previously held by men to keep our war effort viable. It was only then United States and the Western civilizations realized what Plato tried to tell the world circa 400 B.C.E.

> *Nothing can be more absurd than the practice that prevails in our country of men and women not following the same pursuits with all their strengths and with one mind, for thus, the state instead of being whole is reduced to half.* —Plato

The Nineteenth Amendment immediately passed after the war and gave women the right to vote in 1920. The myth about male superiority around voting privileges could not endure when women stood beside men and kept our country going during the Great War and a devastating pandemic. Historians noted similar needed social changes occurred during and after WWII, when traditional male jobs lie vacant, and women filled them admirably again.

Once everyone realized that women could have a family and excel in the workforce, the purpose of marriage changed from survival to happiness and self-actualization. This is the reason the divorce rate increased to 50 percent in the Western civilization after WWII and continues to this day. Learning how to have an egalitarian relationship continues to prove challenging after thousands of years of survival-based marriages.

Gender equality is still evolving to where it needs to be but during WWI, the Aircraft Factory created a healthy, even playful workplace for everyone working at the facility. The *Logbook of the Naval Aircraft Association* had group pictures of everyone in each department with positive comments about individual members and inside jokes like a high school yearbook. The following mix of gender and war humor provide a glimpse of the lighthearted work environment at the facility.

RULES FOR STENOGRAPHERS, TYPISTS AND CLERKS, ADDING MACHINE OPERATORS, ETC.

1) Conserve air by eliminating some of the unnecessary conversation.

2) Conserve shoe leather by remaining at your desk; remember you are supposed to be a typist and not a floorwalker.

3) If you are hungry, go out and get something to eat; don't hang around chewing the rag.

4) We have wheatless days and meatless days; let us have feetless days, keep your feet on the floor—not on the desk.

5) Don't acquire the saving habit to such an extent that you go home with a pocket full of postage stamps every day. Just because you write on a machine don't think you have to get light-fingered.

6) If you feel you must exercise your vocal cords during office hours, please sing, hum or whistle something German so that the rest of the office force will have an excuse for bombing your dome with paper weights.

7) Any person or persons having as a part of their lunch Limburger cheese, will kindly adjourn to the roof until the ordeal is over. There is a strong reason for this.

8) If you feel that you must steal a typewriter now and then, please leave the desks, we can get a new typewriter any time but desks are scarce and hard to move.

9) Just because they are using a lot of ammunition in Europe, don't think you have to powder your nose every ten minutes.

10) Make this world safe for democracy; stop throwing milk bottles and other rubbish out of the windows.

11) As Benedict Arnold said in his famous Gettysburg speech: "Eight hours for the men who work, seven hours a day for the Government clerk," twelve hours a day for the female of the species and don't sneak off before quitting time either.

12) Save a loaf a week; just because you've got a crust don't think you can loaf around all day. If you are well bred, don't roll in here with a bun on either.

13) If you feel that you must wipe up the floor with something, use a mop; we need the telephone operators and office boys in our business.

14) Talk is cheap, however, please don't monopolize the office telephones. Occasionally we like to use them for business purposes.

15) You are permitted to work your jaws all you like—chewing gum. If you want to preserve the gum, don't attach it carelessly to desks and chairs—we don't want to get stuck up.

The following poem about what an aircraft girl finds attractive in a man is another interesting example of the playfulness of those working there. So, imagine it is 1919 and you do not know what a gob is. And who might be the gobbiest gob of all? Your answer in the *Logbook* from page 90 follows:

The Gobbiest Gob
Now who in the world is the gobbiest gob?
And just what should a gobby gob be?
And how can a body select just one
From the gobs of gobs that we see?

Oh! they're some of 'em short and they're some of 'em tall
And they're some of 'em thick, some thin,

*And once in a while we see one glum
But a real gobby gob should grin.*

*Their little white hats they wear on their ears
Or the backs of their necks of their noses,
And the number of angles the pancakes assume
Far exceeds what a landsman supposes.*

*A gobby gob's face bears the tan of the sea
And he walks with a nautical swing
His trousers go flop and his elbows project—
His back view's a wonderful thing!*

*He has cool, fighting eyes, and a lilt of a song,
And he kids 'em all, straight down the line—
"Yes! Yes! But the gobbiest?" How can you ask?
The gobbiest gob is—MINE!*

—One of our dandy Aircraft girls
—Who? January 15, 1919

The postcard Art kept in his notebook.

My grandmother and Aunt Dell, I suspect, might not have liked this straight-talking Aircraft girl, and probably would have advised Arthur not to marry her. Speaking of which, it seems Arthur had many dates and kept the postcard shown opposite of three women with the date 5-12-19 written both on the front and back of this photo. Are these three carnival workers or racy pin-up girls? Who knows? Probably no one cared. Everyone had just survived the Great War and the Spanish Influenza. The Roaring Twenties were just around the corner.

The following stories and testimonials must be considered why Art was so happy he was going to be retained when the plant began downsizing to 1,000 employees. For example, a man named Crennan claimed fool's luck was the reason he ended up at the right place (the Naval Aircraft Factory). Crediting the same motives, a half-witted fellow used to look for a lost mule, he continued:

> "At a small town up in New York State they had a mule under municipal ownership, that did all the heavy work for the whole town, such as hauling coal and water etc., and everyone was dependent more or less upon the safety of that mule.
> One morning when they went to get him they found out he had broken out and wandered away during the night, so all turned out and made a thorough search of the surrounding country to find him, but they returned at night without success and they began to feel somewhat alarmed. The next morning, a half-witted boy of the town thought he would try his luck, so he started out and in about five hours he came back leading the mule behind him. They were all greatly pleased and rushed over to him and asked, 'How did you find him?'
>
> 'Why, he said, I just went to where he was last seen, and I says to myself, "Now if I were a jackass where would I go?" and I went there and found him.'"

The *Logbook* included pranks and puns exemplified by this story:

> Has Ennis discovered who took his engine all apart and changed every blessed connection on the machine? What made him the maddest was getting this postal the morning after the machine was stolen.

Mary had a little lamb,
She fed it kerosene,
One day it got too near the fire:
Since then it's not benzine.
—Crossen

The Logbook of the Naval Aircraft Factory (NAF) concluded with testimonials from the servicemen and women. A few of them are included below:

- *It is written in our recollection with marks that fade not, how fine it was to serve at the NAF.*
- *The Americans at the NAF were blue-blooded aristocratic democrats, with red blood in their veins, and white ways.*
- *The NAF membership—the finest lot of men sifted together into a heap of usefulness.*
- *Let us cherish the kindly memory of the splendid spirit of good fellowship, co-operation and democracy found throughout the NAF.*
- *The NAF boys were the finest bunch of men in all the world.*
- *Production is not produced with theories and dreams. A little NAF kind of work makes a C-1 rise from pencil sketch and soar above the ruffling sea of clouds.*
- *Let's make the aircraft industry the greatest in the world.*

Arthur E. Ehrke's tombstone, Forest Home Cemetery
Milwaukee, Wisconsin
(Photo by Nadine Sobottka)

Arthur Ehrke (1899-1919).

EPILOGUE

Photographs, letters, and telegrams kept loved ones in touch a century ago. Letters were cherished and reread repeatedly until the next one arrived from the postman. My uncle died in 1919 but his wishes, hopes, and dreams endure through his loving correspondence and photos. These letters touch our heart because they reveal family values, universal principles, and dedicated service. Philosophers say our eyes are the window to the soul, but these letters provide a similar view into Arthur's passionate heart a century ago during a gentler time in our country's aviation history.

Writing this book allowed me to meet Arthur E. Ehrke in the same way my family knew him after he enlisted in the Navy over a century ago.

Looking back, my father Walter had similar traits to his brother's. Walter Ehrke started as a stock boy in the wholesale drug industry and retired as vice-president of the same company fifty years later. When I worked at the Yahr-Lange Drug Company in high school and college, I saw first-hand how everyone in the company loved him and respected his leadership.

At the end of his career, Walter Ehrke was mentioned in the *Who's Who of America* for his pioneering work with IBM, which computerized the purchasing process for the wholesale drug industry. I remember asking my dad how he came up with his innovative ideas that led to IBM's partnership with is company.

"I'm basically a lazy man," he said adding "I always think of the easiest way to do something."

"Aren't you afraid you will run out of ideas?" I inquired.

"I have new ideas every day, frankly...I can't stop them," was his reply.

The Yahr-Lange Wholesale Drug Company Building in Milwaukee, Wisconsin circa 1959
(Courtesy of the Milwaukee Public Library)

Arthur's passion for excellence was shared by my father. I really would have liked to have met Arthur in my lifetime. Hopefully, this book of his letters provides everyone with an opportunity to meet him through his photos and written word.

Arthur obviously worked hard as a mechanic and his notes, some of which I have included in Chapter 4 speak to the meticulous care his machines received. Aunt Dell and Aunt Lilian were also very accomplished at their careers. For example, Lillian (Ehrke) Bostrom was one of the founding members of the Unitarian Universalist Church in Brookfield, Wisconsin and donated over a million dollars to charitable causes in the 1960s. Dell (Ehrke) Hummert was a successful restauranter and my sisters Lauren (Ehrke) Lauritch and Muriel (Ehrke) Stanton loved working for her as waitresses in their youth.

When I told my father I wanted to become a psychotherapist against his wishes, he paused thoughtfully and said "then become the best psychotherapist you can be." Loyalty, excellence, and dedication in everything you do was the gift my brother, sisters, and I received from our family.

Family was important to Arthur, and he created a family away from home at the Naval Airplane Factory. He was well liked and respected wherever he went. His rapid rise to become chief mechanic was impressive. The fact that Commander F.G. Colburn planned to retain Art at the Naval Airplane Factory after the Navy decommissioned him speaks to Arthur's determination. Everyone passes away and factories rise and eventually decay, but the following "Old Aircraft Tune" from the *Naval Aircraft Factory Logbook 1917-1918* reminds us not to forget when aviators walked on wings with a hope and prayer and made the world a better place.

OLD AIRCRAFT TUNE

However sweet the throbbing harp, however skilled the art.
No newborn tune may hope to win warm welcome in the heart.
Like that we give so glad to lilts which played us to the frays—
The old, old tunes of blithesome youth, the tunes of Aircraft days.

What rose or green, what lane or theme, what wings afar to sea,
What racing cloud, what spindrift wind, what bird within a tree,
Can be like those that gave the chant or sunny roundelays
Which made our heart, for daring joy, leap fast in Aircraft days!

This bringer of a ballad goes, but leaves his little song
To roam across the lonely hill, or through the city throng,
Renewing life, its own and ours, by gathering on its ways
Remembrance sweet, in vale or street, of those old Aircraft days.

However throbs the pulsing harp, however sound the strings,
The new found song for us hath not that power of sweeping wings,
Which waft us back to those rare days when life was just delays
While building boats, oh! wonderous boats, the boats
    of Aircraft days.

—by Ben Mac (pen name of John McClure, A.P.S.)

APPENDIX 1
CHRONOLOGY OF ART'S LETTERS WITH SUMMARIES

July 23, 1918: Went to Chicago with Fred to visit Murutzke. Weighs 159 pounds.

Aug. 2, 1918: Guard duty, 25 cents per hour. Financially embarrassed. Three more weeks of school.

Aug. 8, 1918: One week in test shed and then two weeks in blacksmithing and acetylene welding. Got a Service Gillette razor and thanks Della for sending a dollar.

Aug. 27, 1918 Last draft leaving for France on Sept. 15. Art plans to be on it and can't wait.

Sept. 4, 1918 Art achieved first-class rating. "SOL," which means "Save Our Liberty," is shouted out to any slackers who aren't cleaning the barracks properly before inspection.

Sept. 10, 1918 Only six men in his company made first class. Guards are blocking the door, so Art is expecting to ship out any time now.

Sept. 12, 1918 Dell wrote to Art giving him sisterly advice about a girl because she knows what's really going on and Art does not.

Sept. 13, 1918 Wearing three stripes now instead of two. In Camp Luce now, leaving on Monday, Sept. 16, for Philadelphia. On mess duty now.

Sept. 15, 1918 Fred finished school. Whole 15th Reg. quarantined because of the Spanish grippe. Fifteen men died from it. Last day, taking a train to Philly tomorrow.

Sept. 17, 1918 Most all camps quarantined, sick bays filled up and twelve more men died.

Sept. 21, 1918 Train ride to Philadelphia. Slept at YMCA the first night for 35 cents. Transportation was 5 cents.

Sept. 24, 1918 The Spanish influenza is something awful here. Twenty-five have died since Art got there. Delaware River full of seaplanes and Navy boats are camouflaged.

Letters Home from a WWI Seaplane Test Mechanic

Oct. 3, 1918	Made two trips in air so far. Hanging out from waistline. Went up 2,000 feet in rain. Hog Island is the biggest shipyard in the United States.
Oct. 6, 1918	At Y in Philly. 168 pounds now. Pay is $56 if Art goes across. He gets $7 and the rest is saved. Proper clothes are needed if going across. Free admissions to all theaters.
Oct. 21, 1918	Put on subsistence $90 for room and board and $66.50 for pay. Building a transatlantic seaplane in this factory but I'm not supposed to talk about it.
Oct. 24, 1918	Balled out for wrong stationery. Expects to go to Pensacola, Florida. Flight is 2,300 miles stopping at Hampton Roads & Charleston. 3 days but 38 flight hours.
Nov. 14, 1918	Accident. At 2,100 feet, went into a nosedive and crashed. One mechanic died, pilot broke his arm, and Art cut his leg. Don't worry, I'm alright.
Nov. 22, 1918	Recovered from accident. Concerned about his friend who died. Learned how to hold his own among men and the value of money.
Nov. 29, 1918	Got Thanksgiving box. Found a private home for $2 per week. Gives helmet and goggles to Walter. On a new boat and intends to make sure everything is right.
Dec. 5, 1918	Two planes turned over in river. Man caught in propeller cut in two. We're going to test-fly a plane "to see how long it can stay in the air."
Dec. 18, 1918	Flying in the cold. Cut wire caused another crash. Flew non-stop test flight for 1,200 miles. "Air must have been worn out in that 20-mile course."
Dec. 28, 1918	Christmas dinner cost $2.50. Trip to Hampton Roads was 300 miles and took three hours. Coming home in a Chief's uniform.
Jan. 1, 1919	Back from Hampton Roads. Did justice to the care package from home. "So cold, I had to chew tobacco to keep my jaws moving."
Jan. 10, 1919	Sent pictures of boats and crew.
Jan. 31, 1919	Coming home on furlough next month. Mother has the flu. Ship from France with 2,100 men came down the Delaware.

CHAPTER TITLE

Feb. 16, 1919	Fred wrote revealing letter to Della to find out when Art was coming home.
Feb. 22, 1919	Fred writes to Art and want to make sure Della isn't sore.
Feb. 27, 1919	In New York City at the Belmore Hotel assembling a plane for an exhibition. Costs $1.50 a night. Doesn't know how long he'll stay there.
Mar. 11, 1919	New York was nice for ten days, trip was successful. Dirigibles are old stuff.
Mar. 21, 1919	Sending Naval Aircraft Association 1918-19 Logbook home. Costs a lot to stay in New York and now we are commencing our Spring Drive.
Apr. 2, 1919	Family car collided with streetcar. Very cold in Philly.
Spring 1919	Rescues four planes from Cape May. Busy all night in gale conditions.
May 5, 1919	Milwaukee creates its own airfield. Nosedive versus bum landing wisdom.
May 10, 1919	Gave $10 to his mother for her birthday. Doesn't answer Dizzy Wimmer's letters.
May 13, 1919	Gives ATTENTION notice to his parents about worrying too much. He had sent home a picture of a girl he liked.
May 1919	Flying more now and plan to fly to San Diego, California. I'm getting big ideas about staying here after I leave the service.
May 29, 1919	Finger got ripped up by fan pump. Fred got married reactions. Sent picture of a sinking seaplane off in the distance.
June 16, 1919	New uniform without buttons and ratings, $45. Might fly an NC-1 nonstop to Ireland. Was on the boat with senators and congressmen from Washington, DC on an inspection tour of Hog Island. Fred sent picture with his new wife.
June 22, 1919	June 28th is Navy Day in Philadelphia and is a big event with the peace signing. Job promised when he musters out. Sore throat medicine needed.

July 1, 1919	Up 15,000 feet, but air was bumpy on Navy Day. Sham battle. Hit an air pocket, came down in tailspin, and broke machine all up. No one hurt, not more flying.
July 2, 1919	Special delivery notice from mother. Fred had died.
July 4, 1919	Wrote about his feelings about losing his best friend and the $10,000 insurance.
July 12, 1919	Train fare from Milwaukee to Philly, $29.22. Traveling instructions to Della.
July 13, 1919	Thinks he will be mustered soon and some of his friends have left the service.
July 14, 1919	Western Union telegram informing parents of seaplane accident.
July 15, 1919	Western Union telegram informing parents of the search for Arthur.
July 17, 1919	Western Union telegram informing parents that Art's remains leaving tonight.
July 22, 1919	Mr. and Mrs. Cushman, at whose home Art resided, wrote their condolences.
July 25, 1919	American Red Cross district superintendent wrote about Arthur's positive references. He had a premonition that he would die flying with two court-martialed pilots on July 14th.
July 28, 1919	Condolences from the West Allis American Red Cross.
Aug. 15, 1919	A thank-you note from Arthur's mother to Mrs. Cushman at Arthur's rooming house. His parents wanted to learn more information about what had happened.
Aug. 21, 1919	Mr. and Mrs. Cushman wrote a three-page letter providing detailed information about Arthur's last hours, how he jumped from the plane and his unfortunate death.
Oct. 7, 1919	Mr. and Mrs. Cushman provide more information about the court-martialed pilots and Arthur's premonition that he would die the next time he flew with them because of their inability to land a plane.

APPENDIX 2
DR. CAUFFMAN'S ADVICE

An Appeal to MEN

This little book with the following few lines is presented to men. Some who are only half men, others who are men only in name but not in fact. For the purpose of calling attention to the fact that many causes that produce nervous and physical disability exist beyond popular knowledge and also to the remarkable sympathy between the nerves.

It is not only intended as a book for the afflicted, but also for those who are not aware of what the future may bring them. It should be looked upon as a companion and friend, not otherwise.

The following lines have been written for the purpose of imparting some little information on subjects of the greatest importance. The frightful ravages of spermatorrhoea and the dire effects of syphilis are matters which must alarm the most calm and impartial observer.

I treat all special and chronic diseases.

LET ME SHOW YOU THE RESULTS I HAVE OBTAINED

DR. CAUFFMAN
607 Market St.   PHILADELPHIA, PA.

12   DR. CAUFFMAN, SPECIALIST

MAN'S FOLLIES AND THEIR DIRE EFFECTS

Has no one ever given you the key with which to unlock the mysteries and the causes of the long train of physical and mental maladies that afflict a large majority of men?

Will you discard the notions of false modesty so prevalent and advocate the diffusion of knowledge relative to the plain unvarnished facts as to the cause of many insidious diseases which enslave the human race?

Is human life not brief enough to warrant the observance of all the laws which were intended by Nature to contribute to the upbuilding and maintenance of man's mental and physical powers?

Have you carefully respected and obeyed all the rules of life in every particular except that which has been an offense to your body, your mind and to your Creator?

Man's follies underlie the majority of the vast number of the diseases with which he contends.

Sins will expose the guilty, and the evil of today will reap its harvest in the not far distant bye and bye.

It is well to warn not only the young who may be guilty of erroneous habit, but also the middle aged and even those advanced in years, against wrong habits, unnatural practices, and excessive natural pleasures.

Some men withstand the ravages of habit for years, and are attacked suddenly with some consequent malady, while others, if guilty at all, may experience quick and terrible retribution.

If afflicted consult

DR. CAUFFMAN, Specialist,
607 Market St.,
Philadelphia, Pa.

Office hours 9 a. m. to 8 p. m.
Sunday 10 a. m. to 1 p. m. only.

CONSULTATION IS FREE

POWER AND EFFECT OF HABIT

Habits have placed their marks on men in every form, manner and degree.

They stamp and leave their impress on mankind from the cradle to the grave.

Everyone has some habit, be it mild or monstrous.

It has been said that "one might as well be dead as not to have some habit."

This is false reasoning; the finest examples of men are those who have kept themselves free from enslaving habits.

All habits grow like weeds in fertile soil.

This is true of profanity, vulgar talk, laziness, filthy manners, noisy and violent conduct, carelessness, gossip, ugly temper, use of slang and other common habits.

There is a class of habits to which countless thousands have enslaved themselves, that blight the growth, defile the system, and damage the possessor in many grave and various ways; these are the destructive habits.

Such habits as the cigarette, whiskey, opium, cocaine, gambling, etc., are prominent ones in this class, but those which wreck the special powers of nature, pollute the blood, and render a human being an outcast from the society of pure men and women, are those which involve the reproductive system and are classed as secret violation of Nature's laws, impure contact, and immoderate indulgence in gratification of the animal instincts.

From these habits and practices spring mighty floods of sorrow over all the world.

Solitary sin and excessive natural indulgence rob a man of the material needed to sustain the nerve force of his body in the married state. Impure contact poisons the very fountains of life itself.

All habits mark the special weakness of the person in proportion as a particular one gains advantage over that person.

It is proper that mind should rule matter. Habits reverse the order of things. Men permit the body, in innumerable instances,

607 Market St., Philadelphia, Pa. 15

to rule the mind. They permit intellect and brains to be destroyed by bodily forces, which, misused and abused, finally ruin both mind and body.

When a man has let his body and its sordid cravings rule his brain, and the conditions become so extreme that Nature rebels and terrible disease appears, he of course, cannot change the past, but he can repair the damage by turning from error and taking advantage of means and measures of advanced medical science which have been brought into use for such unfortunates, and which will cure and restore him to his place among men.

It is no longer necessary or excusable for those suffering the effects of habit or of blood disease to despond, because expert skill may now be obtained which is capable of producing cures of which several years ago no one ever dreamed.

Success inspires confidence, and this, in turn, makes success absolutely certain. For years I have labored to attain this success, aided by scientific researches, unremitting energy, and conscientious methods. I feel that I have earned my reputation, and can truthfully promise my prospective patients a treatment superior to most others, so call, as consultation and advice is free and invited.

I will give you my honest opinion of your condition and tell you what I can do for you. It then remains with you as to the treatment of your case.

If your case is not curable I will not accept same under any conditions.

Results are what count and I always give my patients the best I can.

CONSULTATION IS FREE

DR. CAUFFMAN, Specialist,
607 Market St.,
Philadelphia, Pa

16 DR. CAUFFMAN, SPECIALIST

THE MONSTER EVIL

Habits are natural and unnatural, and the instinct of any boy or man should and does tell him when he is guilty of an unnatural habit; the conscience tells, but the will power is not sufficient to battle against a harmful habit and which allays animal passion for the time being.

It is a direct violation of Nature's laws, and one reason it holds such sway is that it is practiced in solitude, and the victim is ashamed to acknowledge guilt until the consequence becomes so serious that he is compelled to seek help and a cure of its dire effects.

It pervades the rank and file of all mankind, the high, the low, the rich and the poor, and spares neither sex in its ravages.

Some people think that if they guard the religious side of a child's nature, this will be sufficient to protect from the snares of a vice like this, but not so; some of the worst victims are to be found under the most exact and strict religious training.

A five minutes talk of a father with a son, or of a mother with a daughter, would save many a heart pang, for many a victim sees no wrong in the commencement of that which finally becomes plain to him as a horrible sin.

Nothing should be withheld from the knowledge of rising generations that will prevent the downfall of the physical powers of the human race.

The first sign of male power to produce one of his kind is the flow of vital fluid, but the habit is often learned and practiced long before such sign is manifest.

The effect is a fearful strain on the nerves, which has killed many who never really knew the nature of their complaint.

Heavy losses occur at stool, and the effect is weakening to the whole system.

Cloudy sediment collects in the urine, particularly if allowed to stand for twenty-four hours.

Nervous and Physical Decline becomes manifest, and many conditions mark the in-

607 Market St., Philadelphia, Pa. 17

roads and the habit on the human body, such as — Spermatorrhoea, Impotence, or Lost Manhood, Sexual Incapacity, Exhausted Vitality, Premature Decline of Manhood, Seminal Weakness, Night Losses, General Lassitude, Weakness of the Back, Defective Memory, Confusion of Ideas, Aversion to Society, Despondency, Melancholy, Loss of Energy, Varicocele, trophy or Wasting of Organs, and all manner of Nervous Affections and Diseases.

Pimples sometimes break out on the face and mar the features, the eyes lose their brilliancy, take on a dull, lifeless appearance, become sunken and betray their possessor.

Dark circles appear under the eyes, and the skin loses its glow of health. Sometimes the flesh becomes reduced, and in other cases there is a bloated, flabby condition.

The hair becomes dry and the beard refuses to grow strong and thrifty.

A victim may not have all the symptoms which result from this habit, but the possession of any one or more of these conditions should be sufficient to impel him to get the best of skill, and that can be found at

DR. CAUFFMAN, Specialist,
607 Market St.,
Philadelphia, Pa.

I treat all those conditions which patients dislike to consult their family physician about. Call upon me in strictest confidence.

CONSULTATION IS FREE AND INVITED

Always Keep in Mind
"DELAYS ARE DANGEROUS"

18   DR. CAUFFMAN, SPECIALIST

LOVE, COURTSHIP AND MARRIAGE

All men at some time or another are concerned in Love, Courtship and Marriage.

Few men have attained the mature state without having had a sweetheart.

Have you one, and are you a victim of habit and disease?

Are you trying to conceal from her that you are the victim of either?

If you are worthy and have an affectionate sweetheart, she will make you a better and stronger man.

There is nothing in a man's life like the love of a pure girl or woman. To love one of the opposite sex truly arouses the best qualities in a man.

It is the antidote of Nature for wrong impulses.

She believes in you and trusts you fondly. You are her ideal; she has confidence in you which will never be changed unless you yourself are the cause.

If she discovers that you have hidden something from her that she ought to know, or ought to have known before you ask her to marry you, it is probable that she will change her feeling toward you.

If your physical condition is such that you realize you are no mate for a pure, healthy girl, if you have indulged in vicious habits and excesses, if you have made yourself a slave to that unhallowed sin which makes a man not a man, if your life has been impure, by associating her with you in marriage, you are guilty of a crime against her, unless you have been purified by expert medical skill, and that power has been restored which will continue your natural relations as man and wife.

A man should know exactly what his condition is. He knows what his sweetheart will expect of him when the laws of God and man have made both one.

For this reason it is the duty of every man who hopes some day to have a partner to share his life's joys and sorrows, to take whatever steps are necessary to place his physical condition on such a foundation that happiness will result, and there should be no delay about it either.

607 Market St., Philadelphia, Pa. 19

The girl in question has a certain knowledge of the real affairs of life, and a keenness of insight into the character and condition of the man she loves.

If she has reason to believe that her lover is weak, she will learn to scorn him as an incomplete man.

Of course, you have a great fondness for her society. You love to sit by her, to hold her hand, to press her to your heart, to kiss her sweet lips, and to gaze into her eyes and there read love and confidence.

Do your feelings revolt at the idea and thought of your lack of mental and physical completeness, at the thought of your unworthiness and lost manhood?

Do you fear that the contact of your lips with hers might poison her blood with the virus of specific disease?

The soul-racking tortures which attend the knowledge, on the part of the man, that he is sexually weak, or that his blood is filled with the poison of syphilis, drives some to desperation and suicide.

They feel that there is nothing more in life for them to live for.

Theirs is the keenest misery and sense of disgrace, and it is not uncommon to learn that such have sought the grave as the only remedy.

Mental torture and suicide are both unnecessary and foolish in such cases, because all this can be remedied by expert skill.

There is a cure which has been thoroughly tested and which has brought happiness to many homes, and rendered thousands of marriages possible of complete fulfillment, and led to the possession of healthy and happy children in the household.

The dread of thousands of having sickly and tainted children, or having none, has been dispelled. The home became real, bright, pleasant and restful to the tired man on his return to the influences and surroundings of a happy family after his toil and struggle in the whirl of daily business and labor.

All men who are either victims of habit or of blood disease may be cured ultimately, and association with the opposite sex, whether relative, friend or sweetheart, can

RESULTS OF SECRET SIN

A host of results are due to the sinful secret practice.

The victim does not act like others; prefers to be alone, and retires from the society of his best friends.

Chagrin and self-recognition of his condition make him gloomy and despondent.

He is excited by the least trouble, and by trivial causes that would not be noticed by those who were never guilty of the act.

His disposition may suddenly change from a pleasant mood to one of great vexation and excitement. His parents become nonplused and cannot imagine what may be the matter.

He may grow morose and sordid and appear to be carrying a mountain of sorrow when he should be happy.

His nerve power lessens, and he sometimes acts as if he were in a trance.

His thoughts are far away from his occupation, whatever that may be.

He loses his memory, the heart flutters, and his breath is short. He cannot work or play with the right spirit.

His vital forces gradually wane, and his ambition lags. He has pains in his back and his legs give out.

He is tired when he goes to bed and tired when he arises in the morning.

While asleep his dreams are of an unpleasant or weakening nature.

He cannot fix his attention or his mind on any subject long enough to accomplish anything.

He becomes backward, bashful, and cannot well express his thoughts, even to his chums.

Specks appear before his eyes, and the sight may become affected; roaring noises in the head annoy him, and the hearing becomes impaired.

Clammy and cold organs are a sign of the failing powers.

48   DR. CAUFFMAN, SPECIALIST

PROCRASTINATION IS THE THIEF OF TIME

so lay aside your so-called pride and consult one who thoroughly understands your ailment, and who alone will know your case; in reciprocation find permanent relief for an ailment that has made day a drudgery and night hideous.

MEN

especially those who have been treated elsewhere without obtaining results

COME TO ME

I treat successfully, and at small cost, all private and chronic diseases of men, such as Blood Poison, Varicocele, Hydrocele, Stricture, Loss of Power, Weak Bladder, Pains in Back, Piles and all contracted Private Diseases.

I use the very latest methods such as, Prof. Ehrlich's 606 and 914 Neo-Salvarsan, Gonorrhoea Vaccine and Rheumatic Phylacogen, which guarantee positive results without interference with your work.

DELAYS ARE DANGEROUS.

DON'T DELAY, CALL TODAY

DR. CAUFFMAN

SPECIALIST

607 Market St.,   PHILADELPHIA, PA.

OFFICE HOURS:

Daily 9 a. m. to 8 p. m. Sundays 10 a. m. to 1 p. m. only

APPENDIX 3
ADDITIONAL FAMILY DOCUMENTS

The Ehrke family home in West Allis, Wisconsin in 1919

The following correspondence and documents demonstrate the length of time and the various agencies involved my grandparents needed to contact to resolve the death of their beloved son.

THE RECEIVING SHIP
AT PHILADELPHIA, PA.

FAT/BHS/LWG.

August 4th, 1919

Mrs. G. S. Ehrke,
    4709 Beloit Road,
      West Allis,
        Milwaukee, Wis.

Dear Madam:

    We wrote you on July 17th regarding the disposition of the effects of A. E. Ehrke, late Chief Machinist Mates USNRF, enclosing therein a list of effects.

    These effects may be retained here and sold at auction, and the proceeds of the sale will be credited to his accounts, our in case you desire, the effects will be forwarded you at the above address.

    Information is requested as to whether you want his effects forwarded you or disposition made of them by sale.

    To date no answer has been received from our previous letter.

                Very truly yours,

                B. H. SHEPLEY
              Lieutenant, U.S. Navy.
                Executive Officer.

Arthur's parents had everything shipped home.

APPENDIX 2

```
WESTERN UNION
TELEGRAM
```

Milwaukee, Wisc. Aug.7th, 1919

B. H. Shepley,
Lieutenant, U.S. Navy,
Executive Officer,
The Receiving Ship, Philadelphia, Pa.

Forward all effects ARTHUR EHRKE to his home immediately

                      G A EHRKE
                          4709 Beloit Road
                              West Allis, Wis.

Charge: West Allis 478-L
       G.A. Ehrke,
       4709 Beloit Road,
       West Allis, Wisc.

THE RECEIVING SHIP   FAT/BHS/LWG.
AT PHILADELPHIA, PA.

August 13th, 1919

Mrs. G. A. Ehrke,
    4709 Beloit Road,
        West Allis,
             Milwaukee, Wis.

Madam:

        I am enclosing herewith by registered mail a packet of letters and daily memorandum book, which was the property of G. A. Ehrke, late chief machinist mate, USNRF.

        These are forwarded for whatever disposition you may desire to make.

                          Very truly yours,

                          B. H. SHEPLEY,
                          Lieutenant, U.S.Navy.
                          Executive Officer.

LWG.

THE RECEIVING SHIP
AT PHILADELPHIA, PA.

BHS'JTM

September 2, 1919.

Mr. Gust A. Ehrke,
    4709 Beloit Road,
       West Allis, Wisconsin.

Dear Sir:-

        Replying to your letter of the 25th of August, I beg to advise you that through some mistake the effects of the late Arthur E. Ehrke, Chief Machinist Mate were not forwarded to you until about August 22th, 1919. They should have reached you by this time.

                Very truly yours,

                B.H. Shepley,
                Lieutenant, U.S.Navy,
                Commanding.

APPENDIX 2

SERVICE RECOGNITION BOARD
CAPITOL BUILDING
MADISON, WISCONSIN

EMANUEL L. PHILIPP,
GOVERNOR
ORLANDO HOLWAY,
THE ADJUTANT GENERAL
CHAIRMAN
WILLIAM F. LORENZ,
LATE MAJOR MED. DEPT. U. S. A.
JOHN G. SALSMAN,
LATE MAJOR A. G., U. S. A.
SECRETARY

October 27, 1919.

Mr. Gustav A. Ehrke,
4709 Beloit Road,
West Allis,
Wis.

Dear Sir:-

  Returned herewith is the application for bonus on account of the military service of your son who died in the service.

  This application must be written and executed by the mother of the soldier, and should be returned to this office together with the letter from the Director of the Red Cross if you have no letter or telegram from the Adjutant General of the Army, which certainly must have been sent to you.

  The telegram from the Adjutant General of the Army should be substituted for the Treasury Department letter when you send the new application.

    Yours very truly,

    JNo G Salsman
      Secretary.

JGS.M

SERVICE RECOGNITION BOARD
CAPITOL BUILDING
MADISON, WISCONSIN

EMANUEL L. PHILIPP,
GOVERNOR
ORLANDO HOLWAY,
THE ADJUTANT GENERAL
CHAIRMAN
WILLIAM F. LORENZ,
LATE MAJOR MED. DEPT. U. S. A.
JOHN G. SALSMAN,
LATE MAJOR A. G., U. S. A.
SECRETARY

November 21, 1919.

Mrs. Mathilda Ehrke,
4709 Beloit Road,
West Allis,
Wis.

My Dear Madam;-

    There is returned herewith the document filed as evidence of death in the case of application for the bonus due on account of the military service of a soldier who died in the service.

    Will you kindly execute the affidavit form herewith enclosed, which you will please return at your earliest convenience using the enclosed return envelope.

    On receipt of this affidavit, the claim will be audited, and payment of the amount found due will be made as soon after the date of May 1, 1920 as possible.

    Very respectfully,
    THE SERVICE RECOGNITION BOARD

By   *[signature]*
        Secretary

Appendix 2

SERVICE RECOGNITION BOARD
CAPITOL BUILDING
MADISON, WISCONSIN

EMANUEL L. PHILIPP,
   GOVERNOR
ORLANDO HOLWAY,
   THE ADJUTANT GENERAL,
   CHAIRMAN
WILLIAM F. LORENZ,
   LATE MAJOR MED. DEPT. U. S. A.

JOHN G. SALSMAN,
   LATE MAJOR A. G., U. S. A.
   SECRETARY

July 31, 1920

Mrs. Mathilda Ehrke,
4709 Beloit Rd.,
West Allis, Wisconsin.

        In re: Arthur Ehrke.

My Dear Madam:-

    You are informed that your claim for bonus on account of the services of the above named man has been allowed from May 25, 1918 to July 14, 1919 and his 13 months, 20 days active service computed at the rate of Ten Dollars per month entitles you to One hundred thirty six dollars, sixty seven cents ($136.67)

    Check written in your favor for the above amount should reach you in the course of the next two or three weeks.

            Very respectfully yours,

                      Secretary.

JGS/MB

UNITED STATES VETERANS BUREAU
WASHINGTON
April 23, 1926

IN REPLY REFER TO: FABB
EHRKE, Arthur E.
C-265,030

Mr. Gustave A. Ehrke,
4709 Beloit Road,
West Allis, Wisconsin.

Dear Sir:

      Replying to your inquiry of April 3, 1926, the Bureau is forwarding to you our Form 527, upon which you and your wife may make application for death compensation as surviving dependent parents of this former soldier. Accompanying your application will be required at this time a separate affidavit to be subscribed by both parents setting forth their reason for not having applied for death compensation within five years subsequent to your son's death.

      All future communications relative to this case should bear C number, C-265,030.

      For the director,

Charles E. Mulhearn

CHARLES E. MULHEARN
Assistant director

Encl.
Form 527

APPENDIX 2

VETERANS ADMINISTRATION

WASHINGTON

March 7, 1935

YOUR FILE REFERENCE:

IN REPLY REFER TO: FCAD

Mr. Gustave A. Ehrke,
5619 West Beloit Road,
West Allis, Wisconsin.

EHRKE, Arthur Ernst
XC-265,030

Dear Sir:

    Reference is made to your recent application for the above named veteran's adjusted service credit.

    You are respectfully advised that your claim is under consideration and you will be advised relative thereto in the near future.

    All future communications relative to this case should show the veteran's name and refer to the number XC-265,030.

    Respectfully,

H. L. McCoy
H. L. McCOY,
Director of Insurance.

In reply address not the signer of
this letter, but Bureau of Navigation,
Navy Department, Washington, D. C.
Refer to No. Nav-642-8-EMA
140-28-59

NAVY DEPARTMENT
BUREAU OF NAVIGATION
WASHINGTON, D. C.

29 March 1935.

SUBJECT: EHRKE, Arthur Ernest, C.M.M., USNR (Deceased)
           Adjusted Compensation.

My dear Mr. Ehrke:

    No action will be taken on your application for adjusted compensation as father of the subject named man which was received on 2 January 1935 as it is a duplicate claim. Records show you filed application number 348,275 in December 1924 and that claim was certified to the Veterans Administration on 19 February 1925 for final adjudication.

    If your claim has not been settled, you should communicate with the Veterans Administration, Washington, D.C., giving reference to application number 348,275 as that office is charged by law with the payment of cash benefits conferred by the World War Adjusted Compensation Act.

Sincerely yours,

ADJUSTED COMPENSATION BRANCH.

Gustav A. Ehrke,
  5619 West Beloit Road,
    West Allis,
      Wisconsin.

APPENDIX 2

VETERANS ADMINISTRATION

WASHINGTON

October 28, 1935

YOUR FILE REFERENCE:

IN REPLY REFER TO: FCB

Mrs. Mathilda Ehrke
5619 West Beloit Road
West Allis, Wisconsin

EHRKE, Arthur Ernst
XC-265 030

Dear Madam:

Reference is made to the evidence submitted by you in support of your claim for the adjusted compensation of the above named deceased veteran.

The baptismal record as evidence of your age states the name of the child baptised as Caroline Emilie Mathilde, and inasmuch as your claim for adjusted compensation was filed under the name of Mathilda Ehrke, it is requested that an affidavit be submitted showing whether Caroline Emilie Mathilde, the child born on May 18, 1872 is identical with the person, Mathilda Ehrke, who filed claim as dependent mother of the above named veteran.

Upon receipt of the evidence requested above, further action will be taken.

All future communications relative to this case should show the veteran's name and refer to the number XC-265 030.

Respectfully,

H. L. McCOY
Director of Insurance

VETERANS ADMINISTRATION

WASHINGTON

December 9, 1935.

YOUR FILE REFERENCE

IN REPLY REFER TO FOB

XC- 265 030

EHRKE, Arthur Ernst

Mrs. Mathilda Ehrke,
5619 West Beloit Road,
West Allis, Wisconsin.

Dear Madam:

You are advised that your claim for the benefits conferred by the World War Adjusted Compensation Act as a dependent of the above named deceased veteran has been approved.

The claim approved in your favor amounts in full to $340.00 and will be paid in the manner indicated below:

(1) ~~In one lump sum on or about~~

(2) In ten (10) equal calendar quarterly installments beginning on or about January 1, 1936.

This award represents the total amount of the adjusted service credit of the veteran as certified to the Veterans Administration by the War or Navy Department, which credit is computed on the basis of $1.00 a day for home service and $1.25 a day for oversea service for each day the veteran served in active service in excess of sixty (60) days. The law limits the adjusted service credit of a veteran who had no oversea service to $500.00 and to $625.00 for a veteran who served overseas. If the adjusted service credit amounts to more than $50.00 the same is payable in ten quarterly installments. The insurance features of the Adjusted Compensation Act are applicable only in cases where the veteran himself actually applied for the benefits of the Act.

You should notify the Accounting Division, Finance Service, Veterans Administration, Washington, D. C. promptly of any change of address and all future communications in regard to the claim should refer to the veteran's name and XC-number shown in the caption of this letter.

your baptismal record submitted
in support of your claim is herewith returned.

Respectfully,

H. L. McCoy

Enc. Baptismal record.

H. L. McCOY,
Director of Insurance.

Insurance Form 581—Rev. Mar. 1932
Notice to Dependent that Claim is Approved.

APPENDIX 2

bjm

VETERANS ADMINISTRATION

WASHINGTON

August 4, 1937

YOUR FILE REFERENCE:

Mr. Gustave A. Ehrke
Mrs. Mathilda Ehrke
5619 W. Beloit Road
West Allis, Wisconsin

IN REPLY REFER TO: MBAB-10

XC 265 030

Dear Sir and Madam:

    You are hereby notified that as the father and mother of Arthur Ernest Ehrke whose death was due to service, an award of compensation has been made to you under the provisions of the Act of March 28, 1934 at the monthly rate of $ 15.00 each commencing June 14, 1937.

    The initial amount due you under this award will be forwarded within the near future.

    Payments of to or for a widow will be discontinued upon her remarriage or death. Payments of to or for a child will be discontinued upon reaching the age of marriage or death. Payment of compensation to or for a dependent parent will be discontinued upon death or when actual dependency ceases to exist. Remarriage of a dependent parent may be a bar to the payment of compensation or pension. Payments of to a fiduciary will be discontinued upon his discharge.

    Upon the happening of any of the above contingencies or the CHANGE OF ADDRESS of any person receiving compensation the Veterans Administration must be immediately advised. All future communications with reference to this case must bear the claim number shown in the caption of this letter.

    See the reverse side hereof for penalties for acceptance or use of payments to which you are not entitled.

Respectfully,

E. L. Bailey

E. L. BAILEY,
Director,
Dependents' Claims Service.

Form P-31
Rev. April, 1936

(Over)

ACKNOWLEDGMENTS

To my wife, Nancy Ehrke, who provided valuable editorial guidance for this book and added credits and fine-tuning to the photos. Thank you for your loving support and professional expertise.

My appreciation also goes out to publisher Kira Henschel, who recognized this book's potential many years ago and kept the door open to make this book available for everyone to enjoy.

ABOUT THE AUTHOR

Eric Ehrke. LCSW, LMFT received his Bachelor of Science degree in psychology and Master of Social Work clinical degree at Ohio State University in Columbus, Ohio. A licensed clinical social worker in private practice at the Ommani Center in Pewaukee, Wisconsin, Ehrke recognized early on that modern psychological wisdom, ancient philosophical principles, and complimentary mind/body/spirit approaches lead people to the promise of wholeness. He also served as a student/faculty of the Inner Focus School for Advanced Energy Healing for twelve years.

Letters Home from a WWI Seaplane Test Mechanic: How Arthur Ehrke Lived and Died on the Wings of Aeroplanes was a joy for Eric to write. Researching WWI Navy seaplanes, the Spanish Influenza and the first trans-Atlantic flight was a gift his uncle gave him even though they never met in person. Providing a window into the intimate life of his father's family and fulfilling his mother's inspiration to publish Uncle Art's letters has been an honor and privilege for Eric, while Covid disrupted the world in a similar fashion recently.

Working closely on this book with his wife of thirty-seven years, Nancy Ehrke provided another opportunity for Eric to appreciate the artistic and editorial talent she developed as a project manager throughout her career. Collecting stories from his siblings: Lauren (Ehrke) Lauritch, Muriel (Ehrke) Stanton and Lance Ehrke deepened bonds that were forged by their father, Walter, Aunt Dell and Aunt Lillian, their grandparents and of course Arthur Ehrke himself through his letters.